MAD DOGS

The US Raids on Libya

edited by Mary Kaldor and Paul Anderson

introduced by Mary Kaldor

Pluto Press
in association with European Nuclear Disarmament

First published in 1986 by Pluto Press Limited,
The Works, 105a Torriano Avenue, London NW5 2RX
and Pluto Press Australia Limited, PO BOX 199, Leichhardt,
New South Wales 2040, Australia. Also Pluto Press,
51 Washington Street, Dover, New Hampshire 03820 USA

7 6 5 4 3 2 1

90 89 88 87 86

Set by Rapidset & Design Limited, London WC1
Printed in Great Britain by Cox & Wyman Limited,
Reading, Berkshire

British Library Cataloguing in Publication Data
Mad dogs: the US raids on Libya.
I. Libya – Foreign relations – United States
II. United States – Foreign relations – Libya
I. Kaldor, Mary II. END
327.61'2'073 E183.8.L8

ISBN 0-7453-0196-7

CONTENTS

ACKNOWLEDGEMENTS

This book was written in a week. This was only possible because of the amazing way members of the *END Journal* collective and others rallied to the task.

We want to thank especially Mark Thompson, who received 4,000 words from Italy on his answering machine and translated them within 24 hours; Biddy Martin, who copy edited the whole book in a weekend; John Mepham, who took a heavy load of the editing; Patrick Burke, who read and summarized articles from the West German press; Claire Trevelyan, Irene Williams and June Garson for typing under enormous pressure; Toby Shelley and Kassem Jaafar for informing us about the Middle East; Joshua Robinson for adding up tables; Barbara Einhorn, Bruce Robinson, Andy Brown, Moira Weaver and Giangiacomo Migone for various kinds of editorial and logistical help; and the Armament and Disarmament Information Unit at the University of Sussex for many of our sources. We were also fortunate in being able to make use of the networks established through the Transnational Institute in Amsterdam and the United Nations University Peace and Global Transformation Subprogramme.

Finally, we apologise to friends and families for the suspension of normal life.

CONTRIBUTORS

Edward Thompson is an historian and author. He is a founder member of END. His most recent book is a Penguin Special on Star Wars.

Mary Kaldor is a researcher at Sussex University and the editor of *END Journal*, the magazine of the European Nuclear Disarmament group. Her books include *The Baroque Arsenal* and *The Disintegrating West*.

Malcolm Spaven is a writer and researcher. His book *Fortress Scotland* is published by Pluto (1983).

Ben Lowe is a writer and researcher.

Peter Pringle is Washington correspondent of the *Observer* and author of *The Nuclear Barons* and *SIOP*.

Fiona Weir is organising secretary of END in London.

Richard Falk is Professor of International Law at Princeton University. His books include *The End of World Order* and *Indefensible Weapons*.

Sheena Phillips is information officer for CND in London.

Jamie Dettmer is a journalist on *Tribune*.

Paul Anderson is deputy editor of *END Journal*.

Sanaa Osseiran is a freelance researcher from Lebanon. She was secretary to the MacBride Commission on the Israeli invasion of Lebanon.

Carmine Fotia is the political analyst of *Il Manifesto*, Rome.

Robin Luckham is a Fellow of the Institute of Development Studies at the University of Sussex. He is the author of a book on *The Nigerian Militancy* and several essays on militarism in Africa and the Third World.

INTRODUCTION

Mary Kaldor

At 2am, Libyan time, on Tuesday 15 April, the United States bombed targets in Tripoli and Benghazi, using F-111 bombers from British bases and A-6 attack aircraft from US carriers in the Mediterranean. The targets included the Aziziya Barracks, where Colonel Gaddafi, the Libyan leader, and his family were sleeping; the Al Jamahiriya barracks, which houses the Muslim league, a paramilitary force of many nationalities 'generally considered a prime pool of terrorist talent'; a couple of airfields; and an 'intelligence-cum-terrorist' centre in the embassy area of Tripoli. Carrier-based F-18 and A-7 aircraft also attacked Libyan anti-aircraft sites. Because France and Spain refused to allow the use of their airspace, the British-based F-111s had to take a journey of 2,800 nautical miles across the Atlantic and through the Gibraltar Straits; they were accompanied by 30 KC-135 tankers and were refuelled several times during the journey. The attack followed two earlier American military strikes against Libya, in the Gulf of Sidra in 1981 and again in March 1986.

Despite the American claim to have caused minimum 'collateral damage' – a euphemism for civilian casualties – the world's TV viewers witnessed horrifying pictures of the dead and wounded. Reasonably reliable estimates at present suggest 39 dead and over 90 injured in Tripoli and 24 dead in Benghazi. The dead included Colonel Gaddafi's 18-month-old adopted daughter; two of his sons were wounded. Several ordinary houses were demolished and the French, Austrian and Finnish embassies were damaged. Only Britain, Canada and Israel supported the US raid. It was widely condemned in European and Arab capitals, by members of the Non-Aligned Movement meeting in Delhi, and by the United Nations Security Council. In Europe and the Middle East, there were demonstrations in major cities and at US bases.

The raids were truly a unilateral act. In Korea in 1950, the United States had the formal support of the United Nations. In Vietnam, it could call upon the support of NATO and ANZUS. In Libya, it acted alone, or almost. The raids exposed the vulnerability of the world to the whims of one individual in the White House in Washington DC.

This book is an attempt to explore the implications of the new American unilateralism. It was written hastily within two weeks of the raids and inevitably reflects the emotions which surrounded the event. The world may look very different when the book is published and read. The anger of the raids may have faded or it may have been overtaken by new events; further raids on Libya or even raids on Syria and Iran are all possible. Nevertheless, a sense of the current mood, the immediate interpretations of those who opposed the raids and the questions raised about how to contain both terrorism and US military adventurism, will, we hope, contribute to what is likely to be a long debate about escalating violence in the world.

The United States explained the raids as 'self-defence' against terrorism sponsored by the Libyan government. In particular, they were said to be a direct response to the bombing of a West Berlin disco in which one American serviceman and one Turkish woman were killed. The United States claimed it had direct evidence of the Libyan role in the bombing and also evidence of planned Libyan attacks in ten other countries. Libyan involvement in the hideous attacks on Rome and Vienna airports in December 1985 were also cited as reasons for the raid.

No doubt there is some truth in these allegations, but military action does not seem to be a particularly appropriate response. On the contrary, the raids were followed by increased threats against the lives of British and American citizens. Radio Tripoli, the day after the raid, broadcast an appeal to all Arabs to 'kill every American, civilian or military, without mercy and ruthlessly and without any compassion pursue them everywhere'. Murder and bomb attacks against Britain and the United States are increasingly reported in a number of different countries. Moreover, Libya is not the only state to sponsor terrorism. In the Middle East, Syria and Iran are also involved. Indeed, state-sponsored terrorism has come to be almost part of modern international conduct. Taken to its logical conclusion, the American approach is a recipe for global war. The United States itself sponsors terrorism in Nicaragua and Angola. France sponsored terrorism in New Zealand when it sank the *Rainbow Warrior*. Should the Sandinistas bomb Washington and injure Pattie or Nancy? Should New Zealand attack the Elysée Palace?

The inadequacy of the American explanation may be due to the fact that the Libyan airstrike was not about terrorism at all. It was about the global role of the US. It was about the exercise of military power, and the reassertion of a dominant American position, especially *vis-à-vis* its European allies and the Third World. 'What is clear,' said US Secretary of State George Shultz immediately after the strike, 'is that the US will take military action under certain circumstances. That's established. That's very important.' A theme running through this book is that terrorism has come to replace communism as a way of legitimising US military action.

The attack on Libya was the culmination of a series of developments in US foreign policy and military strategy which are intended to increase the visibility and utility of the American arsenal. These include cruise missiles on land and sea; new offensive nuclear and conventional war-fighting strategies; and the Star Wars project which makes war thinkable again because, at least in theory, it protects US territory from retaliation. The raid had many of the hallmarks of the new American Deep Strike strategy for Europe and the Third World which is supposed to demonstrate a greater readiness to use conventional force. This included the use of cluster munitions on Benghazi airport which are said to be 'nuclear equivalent'. These strategic developments are not just the mad Rambo acts of Reagan and his friends; they are a logical consequence of the cosmology of the Cold War and deterrence within which the Reaganites were born and bred. Nuclear deterrence, once the Soviet Union had acquired a retaliatory capacity, always contained the contradiction that it was self-deterring and, therefore, to use the strategists' jargon, not 'credible'. To prove that the threat of nuclear attack was 'credible', military planners had to prove that they were ready to use military force. They had to develop more and more usable weapons and strategies and display more and more readiness to take risks.

There was, moreover, an institutional aspect to this paradox. Deterrence requires the maintenance of an ever-ready military machine, raring to go, as it were. The laboratories which design more and more accurate weapons, the factories which depend on continuous development, the airmen who have been drilled for action, constitute a permanent pressure for the actual use of sophisticated weaponry. The operators of the military machine are not supposed to dwell on the human and political consequences of their behaviour. They are obsessed by the technical complexities of their potential role; they are insulated from people by their high technology cages. The specialist journals and the American press described gleefully the technical achievements of the raid. A headline in *Time* proclaimed the raids to be 'a lethal video game'. The officers responsible for targeting were known as whizzos. And, as if to underline the unreal world inhabited by the whizzos and their collaborators, the raids were named Operation E1 Dorado Canyon.

But beyond even the logical and institutional imperatives of deterrence was a deeply rooted political problem. Deterrence and the permanent Cold War had provided a framework for managing American global power. American policy-makers quite deliberately used the Soviet threat in the late 1940s to explain and legitimise the American role in Western Europe and later in the Third World. The concept of deterrence was drawn from the Second World War and was a perpetual reminder of the dependence of West Europeans, and by implication the world, on the United States. The pseudo-wartime atmosphere generated by deterrence – the solidarity of the allies, the conflation of all totalitarian regimes, the ongoing military readiness – served to maintain cohesion among the advanced industrial countries and to back the political exercise of power in different parts of the world.

As the memory of the Second World War faded, however, and the interests of Western Europe and the United States diverged, the credibility of American military power diminished, especially after Vietnam, and the cosmology was much less capable of underpinning *Pax Americana.* The inability to respond to revolutions in southern Africa and Indochina, or to cope with European defiance, all contributed to a pervasive sense of impotence within the United States. If nobody any longer believes in American military strength, or that the United States is actually ready to use its forces, the fear of war as a form of global discipline collapses. The Reagan administration is attempting to reinvigorate and adapt the prevailing cosmology. Whereas earlier the Cold War provided a basis for consensus among the Western allies, now the United States is adopting a coercive approach. By emphasising new war-fighting strategies, by demonstrating its readiness to use force, the United States is deliberately exposing the dependence of Western Europe, and, in so doing, is drawing Europeans into a more aggressive policy towards the Third World.

This was the significance of the use of British-based F-111s, which was clearly a political decision. The Pentagon's argument that the F-111s have a heavier bomb load and greater precision than the carrier-borne aircraft is very thin, as shown in Malcolm Spaven's chapter. The A-6s have recently been equipped with a new system, known as TRAM (Target Recognition Attack Multisensor), which is just as accurate as the attack system used by the F-111F from Lakenheath and more accurate than the system used by the F-111E from Upper Heyford. The smaller capacity of the A-6 could easily have been compensated for by increasing the number of planes. This might have contributed to more accurate bombing too. The F-111s are notoriously unreliable and unready. They are plagued by a history of mechanical failures, and at least one forced landing, as occurred in Spain, could have been anticipated. If the Pentagon really could not carry out the raid without British F-111s, this is an extraordinary admission of weakness. By using the F-111s, the United States certainly exposed the vulnerability of Britain to American caprice. Mrs Thatcher said that it would have been 'inconceivable' not to have agreed to their use, and that she agreed with 'extreme reluctance'. There is a formula according to which the use of British bases by the United States is a matter for 'joint decision', which was agreed secretly by Churchill and Truman in 1952. But American sources claim that this is meaningless. Britain certainly does not have a physical veto over the use of American bases. Did Mrs Thatcher have to agree because the Americans threatened to use them anyway? In those circumstances, it would have been political suicide not to have agreed; it would have made the peace movement's case. Edward Heath pointed out on television that he refused the use of American bases in the Arab-Israeli war of 1973. But those were still the days of Atlantic consensus, when American hegemony could still be based on consent. That gentlemanly period is over; the United States is attempting to flex its political muscle.

Even if Mrs Thatcher agreed willingly, perhaps because of her debt over the Falklands War or because of that special relationship she enjoys with Ronald Reagan, the point remains. The F-111 bases were placed in Britain secretly. They were never debated or approved in Parliament. Permission to use the bases can be granted by one person, the Prime Minister, without consultation even with the cabinet. And one person can be manipulated. Even though Mrs Thatcher says she consulted the Defence Secretary and the Foreign Secretary, it seems clear that the Foreign Secretary did not know that permission had been granted when he met with EEC foreign ministers the day before the raid. And, at the very moment when the raid was announced, Radio Scotland was broadcasting an interview with the Defence Secretary, George Younger, in which he said that 'my colleagues and I are very dubious as to whether a military strike is the best way of doing this. It is liable to hit the wrong people. It creates other tensions in the area.'

It became clear that, in Britain, there is no democratic control over security policy. And this was true for other Europeans as well, despite their condemnations of the raids, in varying degrees of strength. It is true that France and Spain, who are not members of NATO's military structures, were able to prevent the use of their airspace. (Mitterand later claimed that he had opposed the US military action because it was not strong enough; it was a 'pinprick' attack.) But it has now been confirmed that the tankers used in the operation came from US bases in Spain. Likewise, West German bases may have provided logistical support. The Italians, despite harsh words from Bettino Craxi, were unable to prevent a Libyan attack on the US Navy LORAN station on the island of Lampedusa, which, the Libyans claimed, had provided navigation facilities for the naval aircraft that attacked Libya. (The attack, with two Soviet Scud missiles, failed.) The

Europeans are helpless to prevent further attacks on US bases in Europe, especially in southern Europe. The NATO consensus is shown to be a figleaf.

In every European country, except France, public opinion polls showed massive opposition to the US raid. (It is tempting to explain the French stance in terms of its commitment to an independent deterrent and the similar cosmological logic in which France is trapped.) And yet the official European response is constrained by the commitment to the Atlantic alliance. Lord Carrington, the Secretary-General of NATO, has said that 'the situation in the Atlantic alliance is serious and as bad between Europe and America as I can remember'. Already, European governments have agreed to take stronger diplomatic measures against Libya. This was said to be largely due to a change of heart by West German Foreign Minister Hans-Dietrich Genscher, who feared the consequences of a rift in the Atlantic alliance. US global unilateralism is thus a way of replacing Atlantic consensus with American coercion.

The contradictory position of European governments is, to some extent, shared by the moderate Arab states and this is explored in Sanaa Osseiran's chapter. On the one hand, the raids have fuelled popular anti-Americanism and rallied the Arab states around Gaddafi. On the other hand, the Arab states, like the Europeans, are tied to the United States through a nexus of military and economic relations.

And what of the Soviet Union? At the Geneva Summit, the United States insisted on discussing regional issues and linking them with arms control. The raids on Libya have drawn public attention away from arms control, in which the Soviet Union was emerging as a relatively benign and constructive participant, and towards the Soviet role in supporting those states – Syria, Iran, and Libya – which sponsor terrorism. The period before and after the raid was one in which the United States refused to respond to the Soviet moratorium on testing and announced a series of one hundred nuclear tests. Soon after the raid, Gorbachev renewed an old Soviet proposal to withdraw troops from the Atlantic to the Urals. But these developments were hardly noticed. The United States has provided a new focus for public opinion which can explain and overshadow the lack of progress and lack of US interest in arms control. In fact the Soviet reaction to the US raid has been relatively mild and the Soviet relationship with Libya is, to say the least, ambivalent. There is considerable opposition to the Soviet Union in the Libyan army where officers have been severely punished, including, reportedly, the death sentence for refusing to obey the orders of Soviet advisers. In recent months, the Soviet Union has been slow in supplying spare parts and radar equipment and, according to a report in the *Financial Times*, Libya has called in French and British radar experts to repair Soviet-made radars and even the guidance mechanisms on Soviet anti-aircraft missiles. Before the attack, the Soviet Union is reported to have withdrawn warships from the area and not to have provided satellite information which might have warned the Libyans. (This was also the case during the American attack on the Gulf of Sidra in March 1986, which destroyed two Libyan patrol boats.) Although the Soviet Union has expressed outrage and has sent condolences to Gaddafi, the American action could reduce Soviet influence in Libya still further, because of unwillingness to provide sufficient material support. Hence the United States can, at once, tar the Soviet Union with the terrorist brush and, at the same time, expose the helplessness and weakness of the Soviet giant.

It is interesting to observe the way in which the United States and its supporters are once again appealing to the memory of the Second World War, liberally using the terms deterrence and appeasement. John Whitehead, the Deputy Secretary of State, compared Gaddafi with Hitler. In the 1930s, he said, people considered Hitler as 'that funny little man with a moustache'. In the end he was removed from power only by a world war. 'We see some parallels with Gaddafi – the time to correct the situation is now rather than later.' In effect the Reagan administration is creating a new set of myths around Libya and terrorism. Already, President Reagan is comparing Nicaragua with Libya, complaining that the Sandinistas are harbouring terrorists and that Daniel Ortega had his picture taken with Colonel Gaddafi. He has warned of a 'Libya on our doorstep' (although it is all right for Europeans to have Libya on their doorsteps). Terrorists are bad people who use violence and, quoting Burke, President Reagan has explained that all good people must unite against them. Several chapters in this book describe the build-up of this good-bad approach to the Third World since 1981. Known as the Reagan Doctrine, in material terms, it has involved increased military aid to governments facing radical insurgencies, known as 'terrorism' and to insurgencies against left-wing governments as in Nicaragua, Angola or Afghanistan, known as 'freedom fighters'.

In the Cold War years, Soviet oppression and abuse of human rights was used to legitimise American military power. American military confrontation, in turn, legitimised and squeezed the internal situation in the Eastern bloc, so that repression and arms build-ups fed upon each other. The same could come true of terrorism and military adventurism in the Third World. What happens when terrorism escalates in Europe and America, when, say, a bomb causes serious casualties in central London? Will people remember who started it? Who remembered the Gulf of Sidra incidents in 1981 and 1986, after the Berlin disco bomb?

In other words, terrorism and the Libyan threat are convenient ways to generate a new kind of wartime atmosphere, to mobilise public opinion and to impose allied cohesion. In this world view, the reality of the Libyan role in terrorism is irrelevant. Terrorism, like Soviet tanks or oppression in Eastern Europe, provides a good argument for military action. If there is evidence for it, so much the better. There is no genuine concern about people killed by bombs or about political prisoners; if there were, a different approach would be adopted. Dead Libyans, just like dead Nicaraguans, don't really exist. Gaddafi's children do not appear to evoke a shadow of guilt. Non-Americans are simply not people.

It would, of course, be wrong to treat this as a thought-out strategy. There is a kind of unreality about Reagan and his colleagues. The American senator on BBC TV *Newsnight* on the day of the raid was a good-looking robot; you could see his mind working hard behind the impassive exterior as he listened to the difficult questions raised by the British politicians. They are, as it were, prisoners of their cosmology, creations of the manipulators of public opinion, no longer able to distinguish fantasy from reality. We can see this in the way they have merrily adopted the Star Wars fantasy: 'The force is with us,' says President

Reagan. And that may be part of the prerequisite of power in modern America. To be president you may have to be mad or be an actor. Carter's sanity did not last long.

But the Reaganite assertion of power may not be successful. The extent to which military power, short of nuclear war, can be used to assert political interest is much more limited today than it was in the nineteenth century. It has become incredibly expensive in resources and in lives because of the global spread of sophisticated weaponry. Moreover, if it is to remain popular domestically, it has to stay at the level of psychological spectacle. There is a thin dividing line between the imaginary and the real. The real, as was evident in Vietnam, is difficult to sustain. What would have happened if the Falklands War had not been so quickly successful? But so long as military power remains in the psychological realm, its effectiveness depends on its psychological success. In this respect, the way in which the opposition in Europe evolves is of central importance. A major objective of this book is to contribute to that evolution. The aftermath of Libya does provide an opportunity to reopen the question of US bases in a respectable and even politically effective way. It could also stimulate a new interest in the underlying causes of terrorism and promote an independent European initiative *vis-à-vis* the Middle East. In Britain, in particular, it could also compel the left and the peace movement to address seriously the Irish question. If Europeans reject the connection between terrorism and the exercise of military power, and refuse to be coerced by the new global unilateralism, this in itself could help to unravel the new cosmology.

How far does the American madness go? Libya could be said to have brought us to the brink. Either Western Europe pursues a more independent policy towards the Warsaw Pact countries and the Third World, fostering *détente* and arms limitation, confining and insulating itself from the American madness, or we will be swept up in a new world of terrorism, confrontation and adventurism which can have no foreseeable end.

LETTER TO AMERICANS

E. P. Thompson

Worcester, England
22 April 1986

Dear Americans,

I will explain to you why I am, just now, what you call 'anti-American'.

I have difficulty in being this, since I am, in ethnic origin, half-American myself. When I say this, my American friends think I am making some sort of joke. It is supposed that all nations are 'ethnic' except Americans, who are in some way post-ethnic. Yet if ethnicity comprises historical and cultural traditions, Americans (of whatever colour) are as ethnic as anyone, and are also becoming more nationalistic with each year.

On my mother's side, I can trace American ancestry, along five or six lines, for over 300 years. I have spent pleasant days, reversing the usual genealogical pilgrimage, hunting out simple burial stones of ancestors in Rhode Island field plots.

I'm afraid that most of this ancestry was WASP. My great-great-grandfather, Judge William Jessup, nominated Lincoln at the Chicago Republican Convention and chaired the committee which drew up his campaign platform.

His son, Henry Jessup, was one of the founders of the American Mission in the Lebanon, where my mother was born and grew up. If you read his *Fifty-Three Years in Syria* you will find that there were Americans in those days who did not regard the Islamic world as being made up of 'wogs', 'gooks' or targets for bombardment. (In 1984 the *New Jersey* lobbed half-ton shells on to the hills around Zahle where my mother spent her childhood.)

You will also find out that the troubles of the Middle East did not start yesterday. They were there before the state of Israel. In that tormented human macedoine (the Lebanon), Druse and Maronites, Moslem and Christian sects, warred with each other 150 years ago.

The British and the French in those days sought to reform the manners of the people by indiscriminate acts of retaliation. The British, in 1841, had the brilliant idea of bombarding Beirut. All this did was to prepare for the ferocious retribution which the Druse visited upon Christian villages in the massacres of 1860.

Since the British gave this example of 'diplomacy', I suppose that my British half should congratulate you on following our example. It is the American half of me which rises up in outrage.

What has come over you? What has caused this strange national self-exaltation, this isolationism of the heart, these intrusions upon others' territories and cultures, these Rambo reflexes?

How can a nation which preens itself on its sensitivity to racism in its domestic arrangements behave with brutal racist indifference towards Libyans?

Terrorism is a word for things so terrible that it dulls the brain like alcohol. For the death of one American serviceman in West Berlin – there was also another death, but since it was a Turk and a woman it is rarely mentioned – 63 Libyan lives are exacted. Perhaps there was Libyan involvement in the Berlin disco terror, but no one has yet put that to any jury.

An eye for an eye is questionable morality. But by your moral arithmetic, one American pair of eyes equals the eyes of 63 Libyans. Human blood is precious, but my American ancestry did not teach me that American blood is ten times more valuable than European and one hundred times more valuable than Libyan or Nicaraguan, 'wog' or 'commie' or 'gook' blood.

The harbouring of terrorists is certainly a foul offence. Each year huge sums are collected in the USA to buy arms for the Provisional IRA. At the St Patrick's Day parades in New York City, graced by mayors and political dignitaries, the collectors are out, and no doubt my liberal friends have contributed, with no notion of the anguish which this brings to sectarian-tormented Northern Ireland. It is said that American money may have been used to buy Libyan arms, used for IRA terrorism in Ireland or England. It is being asked very widely in Britain today whether this now entitles us to get out our ageing Vulcan bombers and bomb New York.

Terrorism is infinitely recessive, like Chinese boxes. Where do we start? With the British bombarding Beirut? With the Druse massacres of Christians? With Mr Begin's Stern Gang blowing up the St David Hotel full of Brits? With Israeli bombing strikes on the Lebanon? With CIA-backed adventures, first to install that good anti-communist, Gaddafi, and then to assassinate him when he turned out to be less pliant? With the drowning by American gunfire of Libyan sailors in the Gulf of Sidra? With the Berlin disco? Or with the state terrorism – and assassination attempt – of your F-111s on Tripoli?

What Druse massacre of the future is now being meditated in darkening hearts throughout the Islamic world? Is it true (as we have been told) that not one voice has yet been heard in Congress, explicitly condemning the terror bombing of the sleeping city of Tripoli? Are all the compassionate and internationally minded Americans whom I used to know now dead? And do their descendants not care?

If my American half feels outrage against my motherland, my British (or European) half regards my fatherland with shame. Those F-111s were launched from the English countryside. You have been told that, while other Europeans are wimps, Mrs Thatcher is a heroine who 'walks tall'. I can assure you that she is no heroine to her own people. She is seen as the betrayer of our national integrity and our national honour. Our land has been used to harbour your state terrorism, in exactly the same way as the Libyans are accused of harbouring Palestinian agents. The feelings of two-thirds of our nation are those of revulsion and shame, not of fear. To be sure, there is a not-unnatural dislike of the immediate consequences. At a time when the Archbishop of Canterbury's representative, Mr Terry Waite, has been, at risk to his own life, patiently negotiating the release of American hostages in the Lebanon, your actions have caused the murder of British hostages and turmoil at European airports and sensitive points – which are nearer to the Islamic world than your own.

We understand that Americans, having done their worst to screw our world up, will now abstain from taking their holidays in Europe for fear that they might get hurt. But we are slow to learn our right place, and have not yet concurred in your low valuation of European blood.

There are also – if I may impose on your patience a little longer, as you prepare to take holidays in the safety of Russia and China – some small political objections. Many Europeans don't like US policies in Central America, but we watch them with the resignation proper to our station. After all, you've been going on like that for a century or so. And it is 'your' back-yard.

But the Mediterranean is not even Europe's back-yard. It is part of Europe. It is the cradle of European civilisation, and even on its southern shore there are ancient half-European cities, a European diaspora.

It is not your sea and we don't know what you are doing there. Do you? What *are* you doing there? Who invited you? By what right do you blunder and bomb and bombard around its shores?

Don't pretend that something called NATO asked you to do this. It did not. It was not consulted. The NATO allies most closely concerned in that sensitive zone – Spain, Italy and Greece – are appalled.

If you decide to fund and arm terrorists in Nicaragua, maybe that's your own affair, the affair of your victims, and of nations in America, South and North. But if you start bombing around the fringes of Europe, without any consultation with your allies, then NATO is nothing but a hole with an American gun pointing through it.

You have turned my fatherland into the Diego Garcia of the North Atlantic, a launching-base for your state terrorism. Most of my own people agree with me. That is a comfort of sorts. But the comfort will be worth little until your bases have been removed.

That is why both halves of me – the American and the British – unite in what you misrecognise as 'anti-Americanism'. It is because I value American traditions that I am opposed to the public face of the American state, to the cowardly bombast of its reigning politicians, to the evil which its racist aggression is reproducing, and the dangers into which it is leading the whole world. I am not opposed to Americans. I think it is tragic that they have forgotten their traditions and lost their way, through an overdose from their media of ideological alcohol.

People are asking, up and down Europe, whether this or that nation ought now to leave NATO? My own advice leads to a cleaner and simpler solution. Let the European NATO allies, with courtesy and thanks, invite the United States to leave NATO. If she will not leave, then let them expel her. They can then attend to their own security needs in whichever way best suits them, and engage in their own negotiations for disarmament with the Soviet bloc.

We shall certainly feel safer when your F-111s, Poseidons and battle-fleets have gone home. You will probably feel safer also, and suffer from fewer rushes of ideological blood to the head. You might even find it safe to take your holidays in the Mediterranean again. Where all of you, except for President Rambo, will be heartily welcome.

Yours sincerely,
E. P. Thompson

A PIECE OF THE ACTION: THE USE OF US BASES IN BRITAIN

Malcolm Spaven

> It was inconceivable to me that we should refuse United States aircraft and pilots the opportunity to defend their people . . . it would be ridiculous to refuse it.
>
> Margaret Thatcher, 15 April 1986

Although they were evidently intended as an explanation of the *realpolitik* of NATO solidarity, these words form the basis for understanding Thatcher's attachment to the 'special relationship' between Britain and the United States. Refusal to grant permission for UK-based F-111s to bomb Libya would signal a split in the alliance, and would be seen by the US as an act of ingratitude when over 300,000 US troops risked their lives to defend the liberty of Europe. It could have increased US domestic pressure for troop withdrawals from Europe, with its implications for the defence of the West.

According to this view, the US military presence in Europe is an act of altruism, a gift to the people of Europe by a generous ally, but an ally whose magnanimity has certain limits and who demands obligations from its European partners, and particularly from Britain, because of the close post-war relationship between the two countries.

What Mrs Thatcher's words do not indicate is whether there are any circumstances in which Alliance solidarity would not operate, making refusal possible. Nor do they give any indication of whether such a refusal would be accepted by the United States; in other words, whether Britain actually has the power to control the activities of US military forces stationed here.

The bombing of Libya has placed the Anglo-US 'special relationship' in the spotlight. Did Britain have to say yes? Were the military rationales advanced by the US President examined sufficiently critically by the British government? What are the implications for the control of US military forces in Britain?

Was British involvement militarily necessary?

The justification for British involvement in bombing Libya has been that only the USAF's British-based F-111s possessed the technical capacity for precision night bombing of highly specific targets, with minimal civilian casualties and risk to US pilots. In the days and weeks following the raids, statements by Thatcher made it clear that she accepted this argument, put to her by Reagan, without question. But was this argument justifiable, even on technical grounds?

The US Air Force has 160 F-111s based in Britain, and a further 130 in the USA. But only the most modern versions of these, the 84 F-111Fs of the 48th Tactical Fighter Wing (TFW) at Lakenheath in Suffolk, have the capability for highly accurate bombing at night. As for the rest of the F-111 fleet, the commander of USAF Tactical Air Command, General Jerome O'Malley, told a US military journal in January 1985 that 'its radar is decent, but it doesn't give the necessary accuracy to really call it a true night capability against pinpoint targets'.

So it was the F-111Fs which were used in the raid. Their accuracy depends on a device called 'PAVE TACK', mounted in a pod under the aircraft; it combines a laser target marker with an infra-red video camera, which allows the crew to see the target even at night and in bad weather, and to drop laser-guided bombs which home in on the laser light reflected off the target. These 'smart bombs' can be dropped to an accuracy of a few feet from the target, assuming the technology works without a hitch. That can be a big assumption. Farmers around the practice bombing ranges in Scotland used by F-111s will not have been surprised by the 'collateral damage' caused in Tripoli; on two occasions, in 1980 and 1985, F-111s have dropped practice bombs on to farm buildings nearly a mile off target, narrowly missing civilians, and local Tory and SDP MPs have called for the banning of F-111 flights. As Ferdinand Mount put it in the *Daily Telegraph*, 'if this was a "surgical strike", I would not care to have my appendix removed by the US Air Force'.

The F-111F is undoubtedly the best aircraft available to the US

Air Force for night precision bombing. But what about the much-vaunted might of the US Navy? Is it really true that the world's biggest aircraft carriers cannot mount even a limited night attack against a small, disorganised and unprepared enemy, without calling in the Air Force? Did the two carriers have aircraft capable of making accurate night attacks, and if so, did they use them?

The main night-attack capability on US Navy aircraft carriers is the A-6E. In 1984, US Secretary of the Navy John Lehman described this aircraft as 'the best all-weather precision bomber in the world', while the Deputy Chief of Naval Operations (Air Warfare) told a Congressional committee that it 'provides a long-range all-weather medium attack capability second to none'. Like 'PAVE TACK' in the F-111F, the A-6's night precision bombing is made possible by a combined laser/infra-red targetting pod, called TRAM – Target Recognition Attack Multi-sensor. Used in combination with laser-guided bombs, this system can achieve bombing accuracy similar to the PAVE TACK-equipped F-111s, but it appears that none of the 14 attacking A-6s used laser-guided bombs. Also available on the two carriers were two types of 'light attack' aircraft – more than 20 A-7Es on the *America*, and 48 F-18s on the *Coral Sea*. The A-7Es carry a forward-looking infra-red (FLIR) pod which, again according to the Deputy Chief of Naval Operations, gives them 'a first-pass visual attack capability at night with a bombing accuracy twice that which can be achieved by radar weapon delivery'. They can also carry laser-guided bombs. Despite this, no A-7s were used in the bombing attacks. Nor were any F-18s used, although they have 'greater capability than the A-7 in all-weather conditions', their air-to-ground weapons delivery system has been described as 'extremely accurate' and 'the best in the Navy', and they can also carry a wide range of laser-guided bombs.

The table below summarises the numbers of attack aircraft available on the two carriers at the time of the raids on Libya, and how many were used to attack the two targets in Benghazi (all the targets in Tripoli were assigned to the F-111s). While all available A-6s appear to have been used, as many as 25 A-7s and F-18s were left on deck. Had these spare aircraft been used to attack the larger targets (such as the two airfields and the Sidi Bilal training area), the A-6s could have been used for the two precision targets, obviating entirely the need for F-111s.

The official Pentagon line on why F-111s were used instead of conducting an all-Navy operation is that carrier-based aircraft 'could not have conducted a co-ordinated, simultaneous strike on five targets' – two consecutive missions would have been necessary. But another 'senior military official' told *Aviation Week* shortly after the attacks that 'the Navy's carrier aircraft could have hit all the Libyan targets at the same time, but they would have been tight on assets'.

Type	*Total number on strength*	*No. available for operations*[1]	*Number actually used*	
			Bombing	*Other roles*
A-6	20	14	14	–
A-7	24	16	–	6[2]
F/A-18	48	33	–	18[3]

1 Assuming a 70% Full Mission Capable rate, i.e. three out of every ten aircraft unable to fly due to maintenance.
2 SAM suppression.
3 Six for anti-radar strikes, twelve for fighter cover.

The other military options

Let us assume for the moment that the official line is correct – that, firstly, 63 carrier-based attack aircraft, all capable of launching night attacks with precision-guided bombs, was an insufficient force to attack five targets simultaneously; and, secondly, that it was militarily essential to mount a single co-ordinated strike rather than two consecutive attacks. Were the UK-based F-111s the only practical means available?

The answer is no. There were at least four military alternatives.

Firstly, a third aircraft carrier could have been called in. When planning began in December 1985 for the latest military actions against Libya, it was decided to involve only two carriers in the operations to cross Gaddafi's 'Line of Death' and challenge Libyan radar and missile sites; but when these plans were reviewed by senior US naval officers and by Admiral William Crowe, Chairman of the US Joint Chiefs of Staff, it was decided that more firepower was needed. The decision was taken to bring in a third carrier. So for the very limited actions against patrol boats, radars and missile sites on 24/25 March – dubbed 'Operation Prairie Fire' – the Sixth Fleet had a massive force available, as big as would be deployed in the Mediterranean in wartime. After these actions, the *Saratoga* left for its home port in Florida in the week prior to the strikes on Tripoli and Benghazi. The *Coral Sea*, which had also been due to return to the USA before 14 April, was held in the Mediterranean.

Why, then, did the Pentagon not order a third carrier into the Mediterranean again to take part in the Tripoli/Benghazi strikes, instead of involving F-111s? According to *Time* magazine 'there was not sufficient time' to order the *Saratoga* back to join the *America* and the *Coral Sea*. This argument does not stand up. Although shortages of weapons, spares and aircraft have meant that only eight of the US Navy's fourteen carriers can be put to sea at once, this limitation has been largely overcome by the introduction of 'Flexops' – a new system of flexible deployment planning for US Navy vessels – and by generally increasing the 'operational tempo' (the proportion of time spent at sea, on high states of alert, ready to engage in combat). Overall, the US Navy's operational tempo is now some 20% higher than it was during the Vietnam War, and 'Flexops' means that, rather than being tied to predetermined patrol areas, or even to particular oceans, aircraft carriers and other vessels can now be sent to the far corners of the world at very short notice. In 1983 the revived battleship *New Jersey* was moved swiftly from 'show of force' deployments off Nicaragua, operating with both the Pacific and Atlantic Fleets, to the eastern Mediterranean, where it shelled guerrilla positions in the hills behind Beirut. The realities of 'Flexops' were demonstrated at the end of April when the carrier *Enterprise*, which is assigned to the Pacific Fleet, sailed through the Suez Canal to take up duties in the Mediterranean. Nor can it be said that there was insufficient time to plan for the involvement of a third carrier. The decision to strike Tripoli and Benghazi was taken in the National Security Council on 7 April, and there was no imperative to attack on a specific day. The US Navy had carriers operating off the USA and the Gulf, less than a week's steaming time from the Mediterranean. It would not even have been necessary to have a third carrier positioned close to Libya. US Navy Secretary John Lehman told the Committee on Armed Services of the US Senate in March 1984 that 'in our exercises, we are now regularly running strikes 1,500 miles from the carrier with the A-6'. This would allow strikes on Tripoli from a carrier stationed west of the Straits of Gibraltar, or from anywhere in the eastern Mediterranean.

The second option to using F-111s was to reinforce the *America* and the *Coral Sea* with A-6s and other aircraft from other carriers (such as the departing *Saratoga*) or from the United States. The Navy has an overall shortage of A-6s, but has been using US Marine Corps A-6s, which are identical, to fill any gaps on board carriers. Marine Corps EA-6Bs (the electronic warfare version of the A-6) were in fact deployed on the *America* during the attacks on Libya, and there is no reason why extra A-6s could not also have been flown on to one of the carriers.

Deployment of A-6s direct from the USA to augment the carriers' air wings would make much more sense than the massive effort put into flying 32 KC-10 tankers (modified versions of the DC-10 wide-bodied airliner) to Britain, then mounting a 57-aircraft formation to fly the 3000 miles to Tripoli. US Marine Corps A-6 crews are well-used to long air-refuelled deployments from the USA for exercises in such places as Japan and Norway. Moreover, the KC-10 tanker was developed with the capacity to refuel US Navy and Marine Corps aircraft as well as USAF, with the specific intention of allowing the United States to deploy military forces anywhere on the globe without relying heavily on the use of foreign bases. As a high-ranking Navy official put it, 'you need no permission from another country to launch aircraft from a carrier'.

A third option would have been the use of US Air Force B-52s, flying direct from the USA, to bomb the larger targets such as the two airfields. The US Central Command (formerly the Rapid Deployment Force), whose main purpose is to plan for US military intervention in the Middle East and South-West Asia, has two squadrons of B-52s assigned for such conventional bombing missions. Their capability for non-stop transatlantic bombing missions from the US to Egypt and back has been demonstrated in exercises. Reference has been made to the probability that B-52s would not have sufficient accuracy to avoid civilian casualties, but cluster bombs were used by the Navy A-6Es to attack Benghazi airfield, so minimising casualties cannot have been a serious consideration. The main objection to the use of B-52s is much more likely to have been a worry about their image – associated as they are in most people's minds with either Dr Strangelove or carpet bombing in Vietnam.

Finally, the option of 'covert operations' was open to the Pentagon. Secretary of State Shultz referred to this in the aftermath of the raids as a possible option for a second strike, but despite many years of CIA activity in Libya and the major boost to US 'special forces' under the Reagan Administration, no serious consideration seems to have been given to it. Special forces would have had little difficulty in planting bombs on key targets covertly, and getting out of Libya before anyone knew what had happened. Perhaps the key objection to this option was that it did not have the same publicity impact and symbolism as a major airstrike, and that it would not involve any allies.

It is clear that these options were either never seriously considered, or were dismissed at an early stage. Reagan apparently first approached Thatcher about using F-111s from British bases as early as 8 April, the day after the NSC's decision to strike. Evidently, then, the decision to use F-111s was taken right at the start, and since this decision was not based on straight military criteria, what were the real reasons?

Getting in on the act

It is now evident that there were two key reasons, neither of them related to military necessity. The first and perhaps most important of these is inter-service rivalry. As outlined above, the US Navy usually gets the lion's share of combat experience in peacetime – such as Lebanon, Grenada and the earlier operations off Libya. Not only do military commanders place a premium on the training value of this combat experience, but it serves as a proving ground for weapons and equipment.

While most US Navy pilots spend much of their time operating on high states of alert and engaging in 'show of force' deployments around the globe, F-111 crews in Britain are largely limited to regular and routine low-level sorties to practice bombing ranges off the north of Scotland where, as one member of the 48th TFW put it, they 'bomb the shit out of some little island'. Overseas or out-of-area deployments are unusual, so the Libyan attack provided a useful opportunity to boost the morale of the F-111 crews and test the ability of F-111s to make long deployments to previously unknown targets and bomb them accurately. A Pentagon official told *Aviation Week* that 'the Libyan attack provided a good proving ground for the F-111s to be flown in the Mediterranean . . . understandably, after the all-Navy action in Libya last month, the Air Force wanted a piece of the action'.

The 'proving ground' argument was also given a major boost by the fact that Libya has large numbers of Soviet-built weapons; engaging them in limited combat would give US forces experience in employing electronic countermeasures and untested new weapons, and assessing the performance of Soviet weaponry. During 'Operation Prairie Fire' in late March, US Navy A-7s were used to provoke the Libyans into firing their newly deployed SA-5 anti-aircraft missiles. The SA-5 is not a new missile – it has been in service in the USSR and Eastern Europe since the early 1970s – but US forces have never been able to monitor an operational firing of this missile. Their deployment in Libya offered a unique opportunity to assess the weapon's capabilities, and subsequently to test out the Navy's new HARM anti-radar missile, which had come in for a lot of criticism in Congress.

The proving ground of 'El Dorado Canyon' also came at a convenient time of year. Congress was in the middle of its consideration of the Fiscal Year 1987 defence budget requests; military witnesses could wax eloquent about how well the high-tech weaponry worked, and how failings in certain areas made it imperative that more money should be spent on new equipment. A Pentagon official noted after the raids that this factor 'was not overlooked by both services as a side benefit to the mission'.

Closely related to the fact that the Air Force wanted a piece of the action was a strong lobby in senior military circles which has been championing the idea of joint-service operations, particularly in the maritime sphere. The prime advocate of this approach is Admiral James Watkins, Chief of Naval Operations. When the Joint Chiefs of Staff sat down in late December to consider the military options against Libya, Watkins pushed for a joint Air Force/Navy operation. Here was a useful opportunity to demonstrate the value of his pet concept to others in the military bureaucracy and to doubters in Congress, even though such an operation might not be the most sensible military operation and would cause political difficulties.

Political intimidation

While the internal politics of the US military were an important spur to the attacks on Libya, the nature and timing of the raid and the use of British-based F-111s obviously had much wider political connotations. Reagan has played on Thatcher's uncritical support for US foreign policy many times, but the desire to bomb Libya presented a unique opportunity; the inevitable British support for the actions could be used as a stick with which to beat America's less staunch European allies and remind them who is really in charge.

Since Reagan came to power, his administration's eagerness to hit Gaddafi has been evident. Deliberately provocative US Navy manoeuvres in the Gulf of Sidra have been a regular occurrence, leading to the shooting down of two Libyan Sukhoi fighters by US Navy F-14s, and to RC-135 spy planes being fired on by the Libyans. But European governments have not shared the Reagan enthusiasm for military action, much to his irritation. What better way, then, to force Europeans to adopt more rigorous measures against Gaddafi than to demonstrate that the USA is quite prepared to launch military strikes which are politically unacceptable to its allies? The inevitable reaction of European governments has been to strengthen their resolve to do something against Gaddafi in order to try to dissuade Reagan from further military strikes – an argument advanced by Foreign Secretary Geoffrey Howe in support of Britain's approval of the raid. But whether this has anything to do with stopping terrorism is another matter.

For Britain, the clear message is that the Reagan version of the 'special relationship' involves unswerving loyalty to US foreign policy, and the use of this relationship to ensure that NATO policy moves in a direction desired by the US. At no stage did America ask Britain or any other European ally for advice on whether the raid should take place at all; British Defence Secretary George Younger noted that 'It wasn't our decision to do it, and we weren't in the position of having to make the decision to do it. If *that* question had been put to us, I don't know quite what response we'd have given.' This use of force for purposes of Alliance management is not new; in a slightly different form, it was used during the years of the 'dual-track' policy leading up to cruise missile deployment in Europe. Cruise missiles were seen as a means of cementing the Alliance by demonstrating the clear links between US forces in Europe and the US strategic nuclear deterrent, thereby signalling the USA's willingness to risk its own territory in Europe's defence. But this strategy was a clear failure, since large sections of West European public opinion saw the deployment of cruise missiles more as a threat than a reassurance, and their deployment created severe political problems not only for the countries where the missiles were deployed but for NATO as a whole. Similarly, it seems likely that the US raid on Libya will create more difficulties for the Alliance than it solves. Lord Carrington, NATO's Secretary-General, said in a worldwide BBC interview on 27 April that, as a result of the attack, 'the situation is as bad between Europe and America as I can remember in the period I have been associated with the Alliance'. Interestingly, he called for the urgent adoption of a procedure by which the US would consult its allies when it wanted to conduct operations, which involved European countries, outside the NATO area. Defence Secretary George Younger has observed that 'one of the principal objectives of our enemies is to divide us. We have clearly shown that we are not to be divided'. The inescapable conclusion is that the indivisibility of US and British foreign policy takes precedence over the political health of NATO itself.

Alliance miscellany

The controversy about British involvement in the attacks on Libya has centred on the permission to use F-111s and tanker aircraft from British bases. But British military forces were also involved. The Ministry of Defence admitted on 17 April that RAF Nimrods at St Mawgan, and possibly Gibraltar, were put on standby to provide search and rescue cover for the F-111s returning from the raid. Military search and rescue services are provided for all comers, without discrimination, but the involvement of the RAF in this case is particularly interesting since the USAF has its own dedicated search and rescue service, with six HC-130 Hercules aircraft and six HH-53 long-range helicopters, based at Woodbridge in Suffolk. Whether the provision of RAF aircraft was requested by the US or was simply a further act of goodwill by the British government remains to be seen. The RAF is also believed to have assisted the attack by providing navigational and radar support from Gibraltar.

Britain was not alone in providing military support. Spain, despite the insistence of Premier Gonzalez that the raid could not use Spanish bases, airspace or facilities for tanker aircraft, *was* militarily involved. The Second Fleet uses the EA-3B electronic intelligence aircraft of US Navy squadron VQ-2, based at Rota in southern Spain, for carrier operations in the Mediterranean and at the time of the raids on 14 April, at least one of these Spanish-based aircraft was operating from the *USS America*. France's and Italy's much-publicised refusals to permit the US attackers to use their airspace may have been less principled than they would like people to think. France has supplied Gaddafi's regime with almost 200 Mirage fighter-bombers, anti-aircraft missiles and helicopters since 1970, while the Libyan Army's air component relies almost entirely on Italian equipment.

The history of US bases

Successive British governments have stressed that the 'overall function' of the US forces in Britain 'is to contribute to NATO's collective defence' and that their presence is 'a major symbol of the United States' commitment to the security of Europe'. But these phrases obscure both the history of the US presence, which pre-dates the formation of NATO in 1949, and the intricacies of the procedures by which US national forces are committed to NATO. Official statements are careful not to say that these US forces are assigned to NATO; in fact, many of them are not. And as the bombing of Tripoli has shown, even officially NATO-assigned US forces in Britain can act outside NATO.

After the Second World War, Attlee's Labour Government was anxious to ensure that the United States, as the emerging dominant economic power in the world, remained committed to the economic and military security of Europe. At the same time, Britain was determined to retain access to American know-how on nuclear weapons. With this in mind, early in 1948 Attlee abandoned Britain's right of veto over any use of atomic weapons by the US – which had been enshrined in the wartime Quebec Agreement – and, later that year, British approval was given for a 'temporary' show-of-force deployment of US Air Force B-29 bombers in Britain during the Berlin Blockade. Within four years, there were 45,000 US personnel at more than 50 bases in Britain. (For detailed analyses of Anglo-US defence relations in this period, see Margaret Gowing, *Independence and Deterrence: Britain and Atomic Energy, 1945-52*, London: Macmillan 1974, 2 vols; Duncan Campbell, *The Unsinkable Aircraft Carrier*, London: Michael Joseph 1984, and Andy Thomas and Ben Lowe, *How Britain Was Sold: Why the US bases came to Britain*, Nottingham/London: Peace News/Housmans 1984.)

In those early days, the bulk of the US presence consisted of heavy strategic bombers and their supporting facilities; and though they were envisaged as a US contribution to defending Europe, they were not assigned to NATO. Nowadays, however, most US forces in Britain are assigned to NATO – that is, they would be handed over from US national command to NATO command at a specified time in the run-up to war, or after war had broken out, and would be used in the defence of Europe. But the extensive ability of these same forces to mount non-NATO operations from Britain is rarely discussed or even acknowledged officially. Former Labour Prime Minister James Callaghan encapsulated the prevailing attitude in the early days of the US Air Force presence in Britain when he told the House of Commons on 17 April 1986 that it 'never occurred to anyone' when US bombers arrived in the UK in 1950 that these aircraft would be used for non-NATO purposes.

NATO or national?

It was not unreasonable for the politicians of 1950 to think in this way, since the US presence consisted solely of strategic bombers and their support. Clearly they would only be used against the USSR, if at all, but nowadays most of the US forces in Britain are designed for tactical, or theatre use; and most have conventional as well as nuclear roles. Even the F-111s, which are usually described as long-range theatre nuclear forces, are assigned mainly to conventional tasks, reflecting the growing importance of conventional capabilities since NATO's adoption of the strategy of 'flexible response' in 1967. The corollary of this trend towards conventional roles is that these forces have become more usable in peacetime or in limited conflicts. Elaborate secret plans exist which set out when specific military units are to be handed over to NATO command. Some, such as the RAF's air defence fighters, are under NATO command even in peacetime, but this does not apply to any US forces in Britain. At the other end of the scale, some US units, such as strategic reconnaissance aircraft and signals intelligence installations, would remain under sole national command, even in wartime. In between these extremes are the many units which would be assigned to NATO at specified numbers of hours, days or weeks after a war alert. But in peacetime, while US forces are deployed here in the overall context of NATO, they are free to be used for any US national purpose.

There are numerous examples of non-NATO use of American forces and bases in Britain, including several occasions when there has been no consultation with the British government. During the 1967 Arab-Israeli war, under the guise of a routine training exercise in Spain, personnel and equipment from the USAF's 66th Tactical Reconnaissance Wing, based at Upper Heyford, were issued with civilian passports and clothing and secretly flown to Israel to take part in Israeli Air Force operations against Egypt, using disguised USAF Phantom reconnaissance planes from a sister unit at Zweibrücken in West Germany. British bases also supported Carter's disastrous hostage rescue attempt in Iran in 1980, with specially adapted C-130 transport planes flying through Mildenhall en route, and KC-135 tankers, also from Mildenhall, refuelling other aircraft on their way to participate in this mission.

When the USAF wanted to double the number of KC-135 tanker planes based in the UK in the late 1970s, the Ministry of Defence launched a glossy publicity campaign to convince the public that the new deployments were necessary. The MoD briefings stated that the new tankers would be supporting NATO-assigned combat aircraft. But soon after the new tankers arrived at Fairford in Gloucestershire, they became responsible for supporting early-warning radar planes in Saudi Arabia, and are regularly used to refuel aircraft en route to Rapid Deployment Force exercises in Oman and Egypt. None of these are NATO functions.

Fairford is also one of four British bases used in recent years by Strategic Air Command B-52 bombers during NATO exercises. Early in 1986, a Parliamentary answer indicated that all B-52s temporarily deployed to Britain were operating in a conventional role, in support of NATO – either maritime reconnaissance or high-level conventional bombing as in the Vietnam War – but events in autumn 1985 indicate that this is something less than the truth. Seven B-52Gs – the largest number ever deployed to Britain at one time – were based at Fairford for over a month; six of these acted as mock Soviet attackers during Exercise Ocean Safari, but following completion of that exercise, three of the aircraft flew to Sidi Slimane air base in Morocco, newly upgraded to support US military intervention in the Middle East. B-52s assigned to the 'Strategic Projection Force' are an important element of this intervention capability. Nor is the use of British-based aircraft against Libya new. In 1983, the USAF sent RC-135 electronic intelligence aircraft from Mildenhall, accompanying AWACS radar planes, to monitor Libyan troop movements close to the Sudanese border. The activities of these and other spy planes have caused political embarrassment in the past. In 1960, Prime Minister Macmillan was put in a delicate spot when, only days after the shooting down of Gary Powers' U-2 spy plane over the Soviet Union and the revelation that similar operations had been conducted from the USAF base at Lakenheath, an RB-47 spy plane operating from Brize Norton was shot down in Soviet territorial waters. In 1982, one of Mildenhall's RC-135 spy planes was noted carrying the silhouettes of five Soviet Sukhoi fighters on its nose – apparently an indication that it had been intercepted five times while attempting to penetrate Soviet airspace. More recently, another Mildenhall-based RC-135 was seen carrying Korean Airlines emblems on either side of the nose – a sick joke, perhaps, about alleged RC-135 involvement in the Soviet shooting down of a Korean Airlines Boeing 747 in September 1983, but possibly with a grain of truth in it.

The US also has several large ground-based signals intelligence installations in Britain, which listen in to radio transmissions and other electronic signals from around the world. NATO has no jurisdiction over these facilities, and the vast bulk of the information they collect is not shared with allies. Weapons and fuel storage facilities available to the US in Britain include a large proportion of US national war-reserve stocks, not available to NATO. So while the mounting of a direct attack by US forces from Britain on a country outside the NATO area has no precedent, the day-to-day operations of American forces in Britain include many non-NATO functions. It would be wrong to suggest that these are necessarily conducted without government approval. Although the Ministry of Defence is not informed about changes in the numbers of US military personnel in the UK except when these are 'major changes . . . associated with changes in operational deployments', major non-NATO activities such as the electronic intelligence operations conducted from Mildenhall are undoubtedly carried out with British government blessing.

Does Britain have a veto?

Both Attlee, and Churchill after him, attempted to extract assurances from the US that any use of the bases, but particularly nuclear operations, would be subject to British government consent. But because of the value placed on the 'special relationship', the Americans were never pressed to codify any such arrangements in the form of a treaty or published agreement. The entire basis of the use of US military forces in Britain over the last 35 years has been a verbal understanding between Truman and Attlee, reaffirmed by Churchill and Truman in a joint communiqué in January 1952, and confirmed by every British government since then:

> Under arrangements made for the common defence, the United States has the use of certain bases in the United Kingdom . . . use of these bases in an emergency would be a

> matter for joint decision by Her Majesty's government and the United States government in the light of circumstances prevailing at the time.

Despite these arrangements, until 1960 there were no procedures for informing the British authorities when US nuclear forces were put on alert. The British government had not been told when, in 1957, a new alert system was introduced which involved US Air Force bombers flying around Britain with live nuclear weapons on board. Nor was the government informed when a major US nuclear alert exercise was held in 1960. Even after the channels for informing Britain of alerts were established, consultation was still not assured. Edward Heath revealed in the Commons in the aftermath of the attacks on Libya that during the 1973 Arab-Israeli War, the Americans approached him for approval to use the British airfield on Cyprus for US military operations in support of Israel. He refused. This, he said, showed that Britain did have a right of veto, and that it worked. But British refusal in this instance was not a particularly bold move; the only European government which did grant facilities for US supply flights to Israel was the right-wing Caetano regime in Portugal. But more importantly, another event during the Yom Kippur War demonstrated the limitations of the 'consultation' process: Heath's government was not informed when the Pentagon placed US nuclear forces on 'Def Con 2', the second highest state of alert, in response to Soviet threats to intervene in the war.

The unreliability and vagueness of the arrangements for consultation over the use of US bases has remained. Early in 1986, Mrs Thatcher could say only that she 'would expect to be informed' when US nuclear forces in Britain were placed on alert. Since the US attacks on Libya, under pressure from political opponents in the Commons she has sought to separate the arrangements for consultation on US use of nuclear weapons from British bases from those relating to non-NATO use of British-based US forces: 'It is clear that we were considering only conventional weapons. Nuclear weapons would require totally different procedures'. George Younger prefigured this line in a radio interview a few days previously when he claimed that, while the use of nuclear weapons would be a matter for 'joint decision', and that no nuclear weapon could be launched from Britain without the permission of the Prime Minister and the US President, the arrangements for approval of non-NATO use of US forces in Britain required only 'consultations'.

This distinction contradicts the many statements made by Thatcher and others before and since the raids on Libya.

> The arrangements are the same as they have been since they were agreed by Mr Attlee and Mr Truman . . . they were renewed when the cruise missile question arose. They require that if the United States wishes to use bases in Britain for operational purposes, it has to seek permission, seek agreement.

Callaghan, Heath and Owen all told the House of Commons in the Libya debate on 16 April that they believed the right of veto existed. But none was able to refer to a document or agreement which set this out. Sir Geoffrey Howe hit the nail on the head later in the debate when he admitted that 'it is not a question of a publishable agreement'. When questioned about the meaning of the phrase 'joint decision', a variety of government officials have refused to endorse the Thatcher view that it amounts to a veto. A Foreign Office official translated the phrase as 'standing arrangements for consultation'; Paul Warnke, former SALT negotiator under Carter, said he 'hadn't the slightest idea' what the phrase meant – 'no piece of paper, no matter how well-intentioned, is going to make any real difference at a time of crisis'. In this case, of course, there is not even a piece of paper.

In 1983, when, as Mrs Thatcher put it, 'the cruise missile question arose' (meaning that she was under considerable pressure to adopt a 'dual key' physical veto over cruise missiles), she attempted to portray the 'joint decision' formula as a *de facto* veto: 'A joint decision on the use of the bases or the missiles would of course be dual control'.

Establishing control

In the event of a future British government refusing permission for a US action outside NATO, could it back up its diplomatic refusal with a physical veto? It has been suggested that the RAF officer who is nominally in charge of each USAF base could intervene to prevent unauthorised US actions. But these officers have no jurisdiction over operational matters; they are there simply to act as 'the Queen's landlord', performing community relations duties and liaising with the Property Services Agency who maintains the buildings. Nor is there any way in which the British air traffic control authorities could stop US aircraft from taking off; they have no right to question the purpose of US military flights, which in any case are under no obligation to file flight plans with the authorities unless they are intending to fly through what is termed 'controlled airspace'.

For nuclear weapons, there is undoubtedly a solution to the veto problem – the installation of an electronic 'dual key' system in which US and British officers simultaneously, but independently, have to insert codes into the missile's arming and guidance systems before it can be launched. This method is already used for the nuclear-capable weapons operated by the British Army in Germany, in which Britain owns and operates the launch vehicle, but the warheads remain under US control.

But the attacks on Libya present new problems. It would be impossible to impose physical limits on conventional operations by US aircraft in this country, and the use of British troops to forestall unilateral US actions would be not only politically unthinkable but militarily impractical. The reality remains that British government control of US military bases must rely on bilateral agreements or treaties, backed up with some degree of trust and respect between the two countries.

In several other NATO countries, bilateral agreements have been reached on US bases which are far more specific, authoritative and legally binding than Britain's 'gentleman's agreement'. Spain renegotiated its bases agreement with the US in 1976, following the death of Franco, and succeeded in removing US nuclear weapons from Spanish soil and reducing the number of American military personnel in Spain. Turkey's 1980 co-operation agreement with the US specifies the exact use of every military base available to the Americans, and precludes any non-NATO use except by separate agreement; Norway and Denmark strictly limit US military activities to temporary training deployments in support of NATO, although both countries now have sizeable stockpiles of US weapons and equipment. Greece has regularly threatened to remove US base facilities, some of which have been used to support US national operations and non-NATO functions, and has even been known to order US aircraft out of the country at short notice.

For any future British government, maintaining the 'special relationship' while negotiating limitations on US military activities in this country would be a difficult task. Precedents exist within NATO for solid and binding agreements which do not rest on 'circumstances prevailing at the time'. But if the US wanted to act outside an openly published agreement restricting it to NATO operations, even such restrictive accords as the US-Turkish deal of 1980 allow it to do so subject to separate agreement between the two governments. The danger is that the US will not sign any deal on control of its bases which does not contain a get-out clause of that sort – which would bring a future British government right back to the square one of 'joint decision in the light of the circumstances prevailing at the time'. Such is the burden of alliance.

EUROPE OR AMERICA: THE BRITISH POLITICAL CONTEXT

Jamie Dettmer

Mrs Thatcher's second term in office has been marked by a series of quite spectacular errors which have weakened the standing of her government and rendered her party susceptible to defeat at the next general election. Strangely, for a Prime Minister who had consistently and successfully projected unflagging and unfailing patriotism, her greatest error in the past few months has been seriously to misjudge the nationalist sentiments of the British electorate.

Until recently, the Prime Minister had been able to sidestep embarrassing issues by cloaking herself in the Union Jack. For instance, allegations made by a national newspaper and by some Labour MPs about the Thatcher family's impropriety on an official tour in Oman failed to cause Mrs Thatcher much damage. She ridiculed the claims with the ringing rejoinder that she was batting for Britain, and clearly most of the electorate accepted her fervent defence. In the big battles as well as the small ones, Mrs Thatcher managed to win through, partly by persuading the bulk of the country that her will was the common will. The miners' strike was successfully portrayed by the government as a patriotic struggle against an enemy within, intent, as the Argentine forces had been, on bringing Britain to its knees.

Who could doubt, then, that she would defend British interests against all foreign powers and competitors without fear or favour? But, over the winter, the Westland affair and the rows over the proposed sale of parts of British Leyland to Ford and parts of Austin Rover to General Motors gave the opposition parties the chance to tug the Union Jack away from Mrs Thatcher.

Her agreement to allow President Reagan to use American F-111 aircraft stationed at British bases to strike at targets in

Tripoli revealed a major gulf between Mrs Thatcher's will and that of the country. Opinion polls taken immediately after the action against Libya showed that two-thirds of the electorate disapproved of the American raid and of Britain's part in it. Undaunted, Mrs Thatcher defended her role stridently in the days following the American raid. On 17 April, in the Commons debate on the crisis, she said:

> Terrorism has to be defeated. Terrorism exploits the natural reluctance of a free society to defend itself in the last resort with arms. Terrorism thrives on appeasement.

This was not just a bellicose speech against the perpetrators of terrorism. She also made it clear that her decision to support President Reagan was intimately related to Britain's 'special relationship' with the United States.

> We also considered the wider implications, including our relations with other countries, and we had to weigh the importance for this country's security of our alliance with the United States and the American role in the defence of Europe.

The day before, Mrs Thatcher emphasised in her statement to the House of Commons the needs of the 'special relationship'. In an exchange with the leader of the Labour Party, who questioned whether the American action had fractured NATO, she replied:

> I disagree totally with the Right Honourable Gentleman. I remind him again that the United States, our staunch ally, keeps over 330,000 troops in Europe to defend the freedom of Europe and that, without the United States and Britain, Europe would not today be free. We must continue to keep that alliance.

At the beginning of the 17 April debate, Mr Kinnock accused Mrs Thatcher of being 'a compliant accomplice rather than a candid ally of the United States President'. He devoted most of his speech to a consideration of the best methods for dealing with terrorism generally and with Colonel Gaddafi's state-sponsored variety in particular. He did not appraise the possible implications for NATO of the attack nor the sharp division which the crisis revealed between the governments of the United States and Britain on the one hand and the European Community on the other. Neither did Denis Healey, Labour's foreign affairs spokesman, who merely touched upon the NATO issue, noting that the crisis had 'divided the Atlantic alliance'. Throughout the debate, few MPs strayed into the inner sanctum of Britain's foreign and defence policy, few delved into the nature of the 'special relationship', and not one MP offered an analysis of the benefits, drawbacks and obligations of the 30-year-old Anglo-American alliance.

Labour MPs may well have wished to avoid the charge of anti-Americanism. Their attacks on America were made mainly on the grounds that the raid would fuel terrorism and not prevent or defeat it, that the raid in itself was terrorism, injuring and killing many innocent people, and that it was no substitute for a Middle East policy on the central problems of the area. Such views were shared by Social Democrats and Liberals and by some Conservatives, notably Edward Heath and Sir Ian Gilmour. Sir Ian interrupted his detailed analysis of American failings in the Middle East with the warning to President Reagan that he couldn't be 'a sheriff in the Middle East and a rustler in Central America'. Other attacks represented Reagan as an unabashed, ignorant cowboy.

The lack of sustained effort to examine the nature of the 'special relationship' meant that Mrs Thatcher did not have to explain why and in what way NATO would have been endangered by Britain's refusal to allow the use of British-based American forces. Various Conservative MPs echoed the Prime Minister. Sir Anthony Buck simply said that if the American request had been declined, 'there would have been a major crisis in NATO and a substantial step towards that which we fear more than anything – a decoupling of the Alliance'. He was not asked to explain this cryptic utterance.

Concern about Anglo-American relations was channelled into questioning about the agreement by Attlee and Truman, confirmed by Truman and Churchill in 1952, governing the use of British-based American forces. Former premiers Edward Heath and James Callaghan insisted that Mrs Thatcher could have declined President Reagan's request. 'Under the terms of the Truman–Attlee agreement,' Mr Callaghan said, 'there is no obligation on the Prime Minister, either moral or implied, that would have required her to give her consent.'

Only two MPs strode into the inner sanctum. The assurances of Mr Heath and Mr Callaghan did not satisfy Labour MP Tony Benn, who questioned whether Mrs Thatcher could have refused. 'We do not know what the agreement states,' he said. 'Is there a provision that where there is an overriding American national interest, British agreement is not required?' he asked, adding, 'I do not know.' Scottish Nationalist Donald Stewart was more brusque:

> It is the fate of all satellite states to be treated with contempt. One may question the attitude of *our country, right or wrong*, but to be asked to swallow *and America, right or wrong* is too much.

He said that during the Cuban missile crisis President Kennedy 'paid no attention' to the then British Prime Minister and that President Reagan paid scant regard to United Kingdom interests when invading Grenada. He dismissed the argument that F-111s were needed in the strike on Libya because of their accurate bombing capability and asserted they were used 'to involve the United Kingdom as an accessory in this crime and blunder'.

Mr Stewart may well have expressed sentiments now shared by a sizeable and growing proportion of the British electorate. A survey carried out in October 1985 by National Opinion Polls found that only 33 per cent of those questioned felt that Britain did indeed still have a worthwhile special relationship with the United States. Asked whether Britain should work more closely with America or with her European allies on security, only 14 per cent favoured America and 45 per cent preferred the Europeans, although 25 per cent wanted to stick with both. National Opinion Polls also found their respondents evenly divided over whether America or the Soviet Union is more sincere in arms control negotiations, with 43 per cent trusting Moscow and 42 per cent convinced of Washington's sincerity. The findings of that October survey have been repeated in other polls. Data collected for the United States government in December 1985 suggested that only 20 per cent of the British electorate trusted Reagan, though the Soviet leader, Gorbachev, scored an even lower five per cent.

Doubts about American leadership and the validity of the 'special relationship' have been tempered by poll findings of majorities in favour of Britain remaining in NATO and of the deployment of American forces in the United Kingdom. It would thus be hasty to rush to the conclusion that the British electorate would be willing to accept a major breach with the United States. The majority in this country still feel reassured by the American presence in both Britain and Europe, but confidence in the 'special relationship' is dwindling. Pro-American newspapers suggest that these doubts are temporary. The *Economist* argued after the American raid that opinion polls 'seldom capture the full picture' and that 'there have been bad patches before' in Anglo-American relations. Their view was that a distinction should be drawn between attitudes to America and Americans on the one hand, and to particular presidents on the other. They cited increased travel to the United States and adoption of American fashion as reflecting our regard for Americans. However, wearing jeans, listening to Tina Turner and watching *Dallas* do not amount to a durable basis for an alliance, and presidents cannot be so easily separated from their voters. The trappings of popular American culture in Britain mask a growing disparity in political interests between the two countries, which the Westland affair highlighted.

Much of the Westland row was concerned with the style of Mrs Thatcher's leadership but, as Michael Heseltine made clear in his resignation speech, it was equally concerned with Britain's relationship with Europe. America was being allowed yet again to buy into Europe's manufacturing capability, yet again being permitted to place the Europeans at a commercial disadvantage. He warned that NATO might be unable to function properly if the process continued and spoke of growing tensions in the European alliance. Resentment increased when news leaked out that the government was considering selling off part of the nationalised car industry to American manufacturers, when, as with

Westland, British and European buyers were available.

The Libyan crisis has done nothing to allay suspicions about the United States. The government's argument that it had to support President Reagan to preserve the alliance is hardly geared to satisfying people already worried about a perceived imbalance in relations. But the polls do not provide politicians with a foreign policy blueprint; they will not help future governments to define the position of Britain between the demands of Washington and the needs of the European Community.

As the economic, political and diplomatic power of the EEC grows, conflicts with Washington will increase. The fate of Westland was a test of the strength of British commitment to a collaborative European defence manufacturing capability, competing with the Americans for markets in the Third World. High technology will be another area of dispute. President Mitterand's Eureka project, the European answer to the high-tech spin-offs from Star Wars, has received only half-hearted backing from the UK, which has hedged its bets and gone in with Star Wars as well.

These problems are causing tensions in all the British political parties. The Westland, BL and Libyan affairs have revealed serious differences between pro-European and pro-American Conservatives. Though all in the Alliance regard the EEC as essential to Britain's future, David Owen seemed more ready than David Steel to risk alienating European partners over Libya, in order to placate the US. The hard left of the Labour Party advocates British withdrawal from the EEC and the removal of all US bases. But party policy at the next election will probably be to stay in the EEC (though demanding major reforms), and to remove only the nuclear bases.

Most Alliance and Labour supporters would prefer more cooperation with Europe than with the United States on industrial and defence policies, but no party has drawn up a clear policy. They all seem to prefer a pragmatic response, using the issue as a stick to beat their parliamentary opponents. Yet the disagreements within the parties are likely to grow, and, if the next election produces a hung parliament, new informal alliances on this issue could be formed across party lines. The choice between Europe and the US cannot be avoided for long.

THE EUROPEAN RESPONSE

Sheena Phillips

Outrage and fear was the European public's immediate reaction to news of the US bombing of Tripoli on Tuesday 15 April. In the UK, members of the peace movement called a round-the-clock protest outside the US Embassy in London and about 2,000 people joined a candlelit vigil outside Downing Street. Demonstrations were held at the four main bases involved in supporting the US bombing – Upper Heyford, Lakenheath, Fairford and Mildenhall – and at various government buildings. In West Germany, about 10,000 people took to the streets, and a Communist Party youth meeting in Italy drew 3,000. There were other protests in Austria, Spain, Greece and Cyprus. That weekend, thousands upon thousands more marched in Bonn, West Berlin, Hamburg, Vienna, London and Barcelona.

The first flush of opinion polls indicated that both in Britain and West Germany large majorities opposed the bombing: 65% in Britain, 75% in West Germany. Initial polls of French people indicated support for the bombing: 66% in favour and 32% against, but 63% approved of the French government's decision not to allow the use of French airspace by US bombers. However, in polls at the end of April the figure opposing the US attack had risen to 56%, with 79% approving the government's decision.

The strength of the public reaction put heavy pressure on Western European governments to justify their actions or responses. It made direct support for the US particularly hard to maintain. The attack on Libya brought to the front pages issues such as the role of US bases in Western Europe and Western European bondage to US foreign policy. This gave a sudden boost to public interest in the peace movement, which was trying to keep alive exactly those issues in the context of continuing deployments of US nuclear weapons in Europe and the provocative 'Star Wars' initiative.

The EEC response

On the international stage, the governments of Western Europe have made their formal responses to the attack chiefly through the European Economic Community. But they have also exposed the lack of 'political consultation' within NATO.

Most people associate the EEC with agricultural policy and budgetary wrangles. But it has recently been improving 'political consultation' between its members. The EEC has debated defence and security issues since 1973 and played a major part in co-ordinating the positions of Western countries in the Helsinki agreements on East–West confidence and security building measures in 1975. But all 12 members of the EEC, except Ireland, are also members of NATO.

Terrorism hit both Western Europe and the EEC's agenda hard in 1985. At a meeting in Italy, a working group of interior and justice ministers (known as the Trevi group) was set up to develop an international strategy on terrorism. In January 1986, following the terrorist bombings of Rome and Vienna airports, EEC foreign ministers met and delivered a long communiqué condemning terrorism. They resolved to ban arms sales to those countries supporting violence, though Libya was not explicitly mentioned, and set up another high-level working group to combat terrorism. But the EEC was reluctant to impose any specific economic sanctions. Britain alone had imposed concrete measures against Libya in 1984. After the killing of policewoman Yvonne Fletcher, outside the Libyan People's Bureau, it had suspended diplomatic relations and export credit guarantees and had banned arms sales to Libya.

The foreign ministers of the EEC met again on 14 April, the day before the US bombing. This meeting was the swiftest EEC response ever to an international crisis, following the US military alert of ships in the Sixth Fleet off the Libyan coast and Libya's threat to counter-attack against southern European members of NATO: 'As the threat this time comes from the North Atlantic Treaty Organisation . . . all south European cities are contained in the Libyan counter-attack plan.' The foreign ministers agreed to reduce Libyan diplomatic and consular staffs in their countries, to restrict the movements of those remaining and to impose stricter visa requirements and procedures. The

January arms ban was reaffirmed. This time, Libya was implicated explicitly in 'supporting terrorism', and the ministers declared that any Libyan attack on Europe would meet with 'a vigorous and appropriate response'.

These measures were little more than tokens. The main significance of the declaration was its concluding statement that the EEC 'underlined the need for restraint on all sides'. Economic sanctions and complete closure of the Libyan People's Bureaux (called for by both Britain and the Netherlands) were rejected. Greece urged the inclusion of a specific reference to the US and the US Sixth Fleet, but this too was rejected.

News of the US bombing the next day brought swift and open criticism from many EEC governments. Italian Prime Minister Bettino Craxi said the attack ran the risk of 'provoking a further explosion of fanaticism, extremism, criminal and suicide actions'. Spain and Greece expressed similar concern about the consequences in the Mediterranean area. The Dutch Prime Minister 'deplored' the action. The Danish Prime Minister criticised the US handling of the situation. The Austrian government said it would not help solve the problem. Hans van den Broek, Dutch Foreign Minister and chair of the EEC Council, deplored the course of events, 'especially as the European Twelve have clearly urged a political solution'. And the Greek government, which has close political relations with Syria, accused those EEC governments which had known on Monday of the planned attack of 'violating the moral rules of political co-operation'. This criticism was directed particularly at Britain, and Belgian Foreign Minister Leo Tindemans demanded an account from Sir Geoffrey Howe of what he had known on the Monday. In fact, three EEC governments – France, Spain and Britain – had been consulted by the US over the weekend about the use of bases and airspace for a possible attack.

But the official West German and French reactions were more guarded. In spite of widespread West German criticism of the bombing, Chancellor Helmut Kohl's formal message expressed 'understanding' of a 'massive emotional reaction on the part of the Americans'. The French government, while expressing firm disapproval of the raid on the grounds that Libya is not the only Middle Eastern country to support terrorism, emphasised that

Europeans should be ready with the right response should Libya move to fulfil its threats against southern Europe.

After the attack, Britain admitted that it had already granted the use of bases on the Monday, but maintained that Sir Geoffrey had not known of a specific US decision to attack. Spain had refused the use of its airspace, but admitted that two F-111s had made emergency landings at the Zaragoza US air base, though without having taken part in the bombing. Six US tanker aircraft used in the attack had been flown from Spain to Britain on 11 April. French President François Mitterand and Prime Minister Jacques Chirac had refused the use of French airspace.

Three further meetings of EEC foreign ministers were held before the end of April. The first, on Thursday 17 April, was another emergency meeting, requested by Greece and held in Paris on the fringe of an OECD ministerial meeting. The meeting neither condoned nor condemned the raid, but considered measures to be submitted to a meeting the following Monday in Luxembourg. These now included some economic sanctions and a set of diplomatic missions to Arab states, the Arab League, representatives of the 101-nation Non-Aligned Movement, the Soviet Union and the United States, all aimed at reducing international tensions.

The emerging line of the British, West German, Italian and Dutch foreign ministers was that stronger action against Libya by the EEC would forestall the need for further military action. Sir Geoffrey Howe said that tough action would have not only a 'warning and deterrent effect on Libya' but would affect 'the perception of the US of the willingness of the democracies in the world to take effective action against terrorism'. This could be read as opposition to further military action and a reassurance to Libya. But his injunction to the EEC to come up with measures that would satisfy the US of the political support of its 'allies' was meant seriously. And it incorporated just a hint that if the EEC had to choose between support for the US or rejection of military force, there would be no choice but the former.

The measures against Libya approved by EEC foreign ministers at the Luxembourg meeting on 21 April are just as unlikely as military action to eliminate the threat of terrorism in Europe. These included further reductions of the eight Libyan diplomatic missions in Western Europe to the 'minimum necessary' (the timing and extent of reductions to be decided on a national basis); confinement of remaining personnel to national capitals; further restrictions on visas; and stricter vetting and surveillance of Libyan students and journalists. Libyans expelled from one EEC country will automatically be excluded from all the others. Trade links are to be reviewed and the EEC butter subsidy (worth about £7 million per year) cancelled; but a boycott of Libyan oil – worth about £6.8 billion of the total Libya–EEC trade of about £9 billion – was rejected. Greece refused to abide by the decisions on the grounds that evidence of Libya's involvement in the Berlin bombing was unsatisfactory.

It is doubtful whether any EEC programme of non-military action against Libya decided by the EEC would carry weight in US decisions to use further military force. Unless the EEC rejects the use of military force in any circumstances, the door is open for the US on the grounds that non-violent means have failed, and for the US still to claim that it has acted on behalf of all Western interests. The British, Italian and French premiers have now all indicated that they would consider supporting or taking military action against Libya or other countries threatening Western Europe. Though they have all in various ways asserted the independence of their decision from the US, it draws them closer to the US position on terrorism and undermines further any peaceful de-escalation of tension.

A final EEC meeting on Libya of justice and interior ministers agreed that the Trevi ministerial group should meet at least every six months and that an international information exchange should be set up and shared with the US. This meshed the EEC still closer to the United States.

NATO snubbed

Formally, the NATO alliance symbolises the strong military and political partnership between North America and Western Europe. In practice, it gives the US great influence over the defence and foreign policies of all its allies. This is wielded partly through formal channels and partly through sheer economic and military weight. In particular, NATO's Supreme Allied Commander Europe (SACEUR), who is responsible for NATO's military planning in Europe, is always an American. General Bernard Rogers, the current SACEUR, is also the Commander in Chief of US forces in Europe, and as such can be given presidential authority to initiate military action without consulting NATO.

The US attack on Libya was not technically a NATO attack. It used weapons launched from US ships and from bases in Britain and Spain governed by bilateral agreements. On 16 April, NATO's Secretary-General, Lord Carrington, emphasised that the US had not tried to involve NATO in the action, but subsequent US rhetoric claimed that the US was acting on behalf of the entire 'civilised' world.

The week before the attack, Lord Carrington, who is after all chairman of NATO's foreign and defence ministerial meetings, had made a speech on US television surprisingly sympathetic to the US, considering that many NATO governments had urged caution.

The terms of the NATO treaty governing mutual assistance in the event of attack do cover attacks on ships or aircraft in or over the Mediterranean – including the launch of Libyan surface-to-air missiles against US aircraft in the Gulf of Sidra in March 1986. Terrorism has also been on the recent agenda of NATO ministers. Before launching the attacks on Tripoli and Benghazi, General Vernon Walters, US Ambassador to the United Nations, visited the West German, British, French and Italian leaders, but it appears that only Mrs Thatcher was privy to the precise plan of attack. The opportunity for 'political consultation' within NATO before the attack was therefore non-existent.

On 15 April, the US ambassador to the North Atlantic Council, NATO's political authority, called an informal meeting of permanent representatives. Further meetings at ambassadorial level were held on 16 and 18 April. But these meetings apart, the dialogue between the US and its 'allies' in the aftermath of the bombing was outside NATO circles.

Reagan's statement that he intended to press for 'a more all-out effort' at the May Tokyo Summit of the seven major economic nations took the issue outside either the EEC or NATO. These six other nations – Britain, Canada, France, Italy, Japan and West Germany – are Reagan's closest political allies.

US conduct after the attack has been a series of bids for political vindication, not a seriously planned campaign against terrorism. NATO governments have been torn between identifying with the US position and taking a more independent stand. All the larger NATO countries have made significant concessions to the US position, leaving the most vocal expression of opposition to the smaller, peripheral allies like Belgium, Spain and Greece.

It could be argued that public protest is futile because the interests of NATO governments in maintaining harmonious relations with the US are too great to undermine. Even in the larger NATO countries, the dividends of alliance with the US are not simply economic. One of the biggest though least tangible payoffs for individual governments in being allied with a rich and powerful nation is securing public confidence. But the Libyan crisis may have sufficiently awakened the general public of Western Europe to the negative consequences of alliance with the US, to shift some basic attitudes to security. Economic interests cannot be shifted so easily, but government attitudes to the US political role in Western Europe will ultimately depend on public support.

EUROPE OR AMERICA: THE ITALIAN POLITICAL CONTEXT

Carmine Fotia
Translated by Mark Thompson

What happens when a traditionally peaceful country has a 'war on its doorstep', to use Italian Prime Minister Bettino Craxi's words about the US raid on Libya? For the first time since the end of World War II, Italy was close to involvement in a war outside its national boundaries. The US raid, followed by the Libyan missile attack on the island of Lampedusa, off the Italian mainland, where the LORAN NATO base is situated, sent shockwaves of fear through the country.

The fear persisted for many days, and it prompted various reflections on:

1. fear of open warfare, and the role of the pacifists/peace movement;
2. the question of NATO;
3. the powerlessness of Europe;
4. the three facets of Italian foreign policy in the Mediterranean;
5. the position of the Italian Communist Party (PCI), the major party of the left in Italy.

1) Italian youth and the peace movements. It has been widely remarked that the only visible reaction to the risk of open war came from students and other young people, demonstrating in cities throughout Italy. Neither the political parties of the left, the unions, nor the cultural and pacifist/peace movement groups called for demonstrations. Does this show a basic lack of awareness or critical shortcomings in the pacifist/peace movement organisation, divided as it is among so many small committees, with no national co-ordination? Yes, perhaps; but there is more to it than this, for pacifist/peace movements were at the demonstrations, represented by women (who often played an essential part in promoting them), workers and PCI activists.

Pietro Folena, leader of the Italian Young Communists' Federation, which sponsored the demonstrations (and which is completely independent of the PCI), offers a persuasive analysis. He claims that this is the first generation of young Italians since 1945 to realize that war is not a 'grand abstract horror' but is 'actually possible', and that every young man could be sent off to fight. So this generation's principled and ethical opposition, which informed the Italian peace movement in the first half of the 1980s, especially in its opposition to the installation of cruise missiles in Sicily, is against 'the war which would send us away to fight'. The young people who packed the student demonstrations last year, dubbed 'the class of 85', were fighting in the front line; they refuted the contentions of numerous middle-aged professors who for years had declared, *ex cathedra*, that the younger generation lacked all political consciousness. They were the sector of the Italian public which was most aware, and – perhaps because they are the most vulnerable in the event of war – they were the ones who showed most determination in their opposition to the 'masters of war' and who carry the more reluctant along in their wake.
2) The question of NATO. These young people may truthfully be said to serve a 'national function' in Italy; for the recent violence in the Mediterranean has shed a harsh, new light on the whole question of Italy's independence in the context of the Atlantic alliance. It is a question that encompasses both the uses and the 'juridical status' of US and NATO bases in Italy, and the degree of sovereignty the Italian government and parliament enjoy, given that the principal partner in the alliance took a decision to strike without consulting the other members.

Throughout mainland Italy there are military bases where no clear distinction can be drawn between the US and NATO, and there is no unambiguous command structure. The question of 'juridical status' is shrouded in secrecy; Parliament has been trying vainly to penetrate those secrets for years, but in vain. They concern the bases, such as Sigonella, for example, where several unpublicised events happened following the hijack of the *Achille Lauro* by a Palestinian terrorist group, apparently masterminded by Abu Abbas. Italian soldiers had to threaten to use arms to prevent US troops from 'kidnapping' the hijackers, who were travelling on an aeroplane under cover of Egyptian diplomatic immunity, in accordance with the agreement between the terrorists and the Italian authorities. This was after US planes had forced the aeroplane to land at Sigonella without prior permission from the Italian authorities.

At his meeting with Reagan after these events, Craxi made known the understanding he had reached with his Foreign Minister, Giulio Andreotti, that the military bases were not to be used 'for purposes other than those of the alliance'. It is not only the more radical sections of the Italian left who worried about sovereignty if the Prime Minister has raised the problem with the American President. Craxi broached it again in his most recent television interview, talking about the possibility of 'renegotiating' the 'status' of some of the bases. Again, the traditionally cautious PCI gave over the first central committee meeting after its recent congress to the call for NATO 'reform', demanding guarantees of autonomy and sovereignty for member states, as well as greater freedom of information between them. Freedom of information is of course a crucial matter, dealing, as it does, with the role of 'intelligence' in national defence systems in this satellite age. I witnessed what happened in Parliament after the Libyan missile attack on Lampedusa when, for a full hour, the government could obtain no reliable information whatsoever. The Senate – the upper house – was debating the American bombing of Tripoli when newsflashes arrived of the two explosions on the island. The debate was suspended, but it was more than an hour before the facts were made available. Meanwhile, I contacted my newspaper (*Il Manifesto*, which is not a paper with great resources at its disposal) and heard that their New York correspondent had informed them that the attack had consisted of two missiles. Our powerful ally over the Atlantic already knew, via satellite-gathered intelligence, exactly what had taken place, while the Italian government knew only that what Craxi later called 'an act of war against Italy' had occurred. In a world where power increasingly depends on controlling information, and where national security is entrusted to knowledge, New York's knowing of the attack for a whole hour before Rome, clearly indicates an explicit objective of subordinating Italy.

3) The powerlessness of Europe. This subordination was applied to all of Europe; no posturing can hide the fact that when the US decided to bomb Libya, the structural delays, difficulties and inconsistencies within Europe were shown in all their tragic enormity. EEC ministers were discussing alternative measures against terrorism when Mrs Thatcher had already authorised the use of British bases for the American reprisals. Will Reagan's lightning strike signal the end of the dream of European unity? (And may this not have been one of its intended effects?) Can Europe really accept Reagan's line, which now makes 'the Arab world' synonymous with 'terrorism'? Can it accept that the Palestinian question – the tragedy of a people without roofs over their heads, let alone legal safeguards – will be solved with bombs? Might it not be that the Israeli raid on the PLO headquarters in Tunisia wrecked Arafat's political leadership? The consequence was a diaspora, with the young men from the refugee camps deprived of solid political and moral guidelines, deprived of hope, ready to let themselves be used by anybody who – like Gaddafi – offered himself as their champion, while pursuing his own obscure plans. Must Europe stand by and watch all this? And even follow the Americans with reprisals of their own? Surely not – unless it wants to turn its southern areas into a battleground. This is why a new coherence, a new sovereignty is urgent for Europe.

4) Italian foreign policy in the Mediterranean. There was a strong smell of political decay in the days following the raid. The Italian government is a coalition of heterogeneous elements from the centre (the Christian Democrats, with a working majority, along with the Liberals, Republicans and Social Democrats) and the left (the Italian Socialist Party). The Socialist Party is led by Bettino Craxi, who has spoken in Parliament of the government's 'non-agreement' with the Americans over their raid on Tripoli. He also condemned Gaddafi's Libya, and issued a diplomatic protest at the bombardment of Lampedusa, warning that Italy would respond with force to any further attack.

This is the government's official line; but in fact there are three distinct strands in its Mediterranean policy. One of these can be identified with Andreotti, a Christian Democrat, who has the weight of the Vatican on his side and supports a policy of friendship, or at least good relations, with the Arab world. The US has supported this policy in the past (Andreotti has recently been reminding us that President Carter used to entrust him with diplomatic missions), but the policy was undermined the moment the US decided to counter the eruption of terrorism in the Middle East with force. Without US backing, the policy looks like a blind alley, wide open to accusations of indulgence towards countries who play host to terrorism. This has put the leader of the Christian Democrats, De Mita, in a difficult position; he is doing his best to persuade everyone that his is still the party which the Americans trust.

At the other end of the spectrum we find Senator Spadolini, Minister of Defence and leader of the Republican Party, who is trying to prove that he is America's best and only true friend. His party was responsible for a government crisis after the *Achille Lauro* affair, because it found the government's Mediterranean policy too lenient to terrorists and too friendly with the Palestinians. Spadolini thinks Italy should side directly with the US in the fight against terrorism; should not deal with the Palestinians; and should promote the idea of a multinational armed force in the Mediterranean, alert and ready to intervene as needed. This approach is associated with a certain frenetic activism and a strong tendency to muscle-flexing (even if, in Italy's case, the muscles are nothing to shout about).

Prime Minister Craxi has skilfully managed to insert himself between the Foreign Minister and the Defence Minister, and combine their policies. He reacted firmly to Sigonella, denouncing the violation of national sovereignty, and has since kept the same general line, speaking against the Defence Minister and expressing Italian disagreement with the strike on Tripoli. At the same time Craxi did not hesitate to lean on Spadolini to help overcome Andreotti's reservations when they had to implement diplomatic measures against Libya and distance themselves from the Gaddafi regime.

Craxi has a thankless task: he must convince the American President that Italy is still a loyal ally, while knowing that American pressure has already destroyed any autonomous Italian initiatives to bring peace to the Mediterranean.

5) The position of the PCI. The consensus of support for Craxi's policy in the PCI, the major opposition party, is significant. The

PCI has sponsored no demonstrations, nor have its spokesmen pronounced on the Libya issue, though a few days after the raid, PCI leader Alessandro Natta spoke against 'American aggression' and called for 'reforms within NATO'. Of course, no one wants to risk looking like a Gaddafi supporter, but perhaps the main reason for the PCI's stance was a question much discussed at its party congress (which ended a few hours before the strike on Tripoli and was, incidentally, a personal triumph for Natta): how the party should develop its relations with the US. The congress rejected positions that were particularly critical of the US, adopting a policy of improving relations with the US Democratic Party. It also supported a policy of orientation towards Europe and the West, while severing ties with the Soviet Union. It approved a description of the party as 'an integral part of the West European left' and as a 'party of reform'.

One must wonder if such prudence may not be overturned by the march of events. One may also hope that the freshness of youthful protest against warmongering will infect even the PCI, which at the moment inclines more to diplomatic measures and parliamentary question-and-answer than to encouraging a peace movement. It is this which is surely indispensable, especially if you want to speak to all men and women, regardless of their politics, religion and ideology. But perhaps there are grounds for hope: was it not the aim and achievement of the PCI's last leader, Enrico Berlinguer, who died in 1984, to encourage the peace movement in all its strength, without neglecting diplomacy?

VIEW FROM WASHINGTON

Peter Pringle

By coincidence, Americans on the east coast were sitting down to watch the nightly seven o'clock television news at the precise moment that US warplanes, in the largest air raid since the Vietnam War, began to hit targets in Libya, where it was two o'clock in the morning. At 7.02.02 (according to NBC TV network, which claimed to have scooped its rivals), the first sounds of the bombing were recorded by American correspondents dangling telephones out of their hotel windows in Tripoli. One says 'by coincidence' because it would seem churlish to consider that the Pentagon had planned its operation to provide *cinema vérité* for the folks back home. Certainly, there are always excellent reasons for attacking at night, and in Libya's case these were telling because Libyan pilots have little experience of night-flying. Yet the coincidence is troubling because there's a popular notion, almost a belief, that few decisions are taken in the White House without considering whether or not they should be released for the mass-audience evening news show. The more popular the decision, the more likely it is to be released. Until the secret attack plans are unlocked, or leaked, it will not be known why the President agreed to set the raid for two in the morning, Libyan time, and not one-thirty, or two-thirty, or three.

What is known can only make us suspicious that the raid was the culmination of a very successful propaganda campaign. We know that if the raid had taken place at one-thirty only one national news programme, ABC, would have been on the air, but that at two o'clock two networks, NBC and CBS, have their half-hour shows watched by millions of people across the nation who evidently loved every second of the 13-minute raid. The sound of the battle – the 24 planes streaking into the attack at nine miles a minute, 400 feet above the ground, and the rat-tat-tat of the anti-aircraft fire was, indeed, the stuff of Rambo. Later, the Pentagon even provided sample voices of the cockpit chatter. 'These bombs are for you, Colonel,' one Biggles-type bombardier is said to have whooped into his intercom as he released his bombs. 'Man, what a target,' a pilot is officially reported to have exclaimed as he lined up his F-111 for a strike on Soviet-made Il-76 cargo planes, squatting on the apron at Tripoli airport. The exultation after the evening news was lusty and prolonged. There is no question that Americans thought their President had done the right thing. Post-attack polls showed that 77% approved of the strike itself, and also of the strategy; Reagan's foreign policy rating shot up from 51% the previous week to 76%. The White House switchboard was flooded with calls congratulating the President, and the British Embassy in Washington took calls thanking Mrs Thatcher for allowing American planes based in Britain to be used in the raid.

If there was a hint of dissatisfaction, it came not, as might have been expected, from the political left, but from the right, who complained that the attack had not gone far enough, that the targets picked were somehow inadequate, that they didn't get the job done, that Gaddafi was still alive. Daniel Pipes, of the Foreign Research Institute in Philadelphia, said, 'The next one should use massive force, anything in between is not effective.' Everyone assumed that the Libyans would strike back with more terrorist attacks, but that didn't matter so much now because the Stars and Stripes were flying proudly again in the Mediterranean, and because Reagan had said he would do it again, and again, if American lives were lost. The President had finally delivered something that many Americans had been waiting for in the painful post-Vietnam period; here was emancipation at last, liberation from servitudes which had rendered the great eagle impotent. Several American commentators noted that two hundred years ago, when merchant ships of the fledgling American republic were being terrorised by the Barbary pirates in the Mediterranean, Thomas Jefferson remarked that the country was 'caught between indignation and impotence'. Others recalled that by historical happenstance the Libyan raid had come exactly 25 years after the United States had sent a ragged armada on a humiliating voyage to the Bay of Pigs. That era had passed. In a chorus of national exultation Americans cried, 'We are not impotent now'.

Reagan had struck an overwhelmingly popular chord, which few are prepared to attack. One searched in vain for congressional voices expressing opposition, even a doubt or two. 'I am sure,' said Ted Kennedy, sidestepping a reporter's question about his own feelings, 'that all Americans will stand with the President.' The *New York Times*, often a stern critic of the administration's foreign policy, rushed into print with an editorial declaring,

> . . . even the most scrupulous citizen can only approve and applaud the American attacks on Libya . . . if there were such a thing as due process in the court of world opinion, the United States has prosecuted and punished [Gaddafi] carefully, proportionately – and justly.

A lone voice in opposition came from an unusual quarter – the *Wall Street Journal*. Alexander Cockburn, in his regular column for the paper, wrote, 'How is it that the Reagan administration could, without any apparent sense of irony, proclaim its duty to wage war on terrorism at the very moment it was seeking millions from Congress to export terrorism via its Contra clients in Nicaragua? How is it that Colonel Gaddafi can be enlarged from a figure of puny consequence into the world's premier contriver of terror? Amnesty International reckons his unfortunate political victims in two figures. Since 1980, more than 50,000 people have died in El Salvador, largely as a result of right-wing violence condoned by the US . . . Where is the sense of proportion?'

Actually, there are plenty of Americans, call them liberals for convenience, who see the irony, understand the disproportionate response, know perfectly well that terrorist acts sponsored by Syria or Iran are likely to be more lethal and more directly aimed at Americans than anything Gaddafi is likely to have a hand in, but they were silenced by the Libyan raid. When, earlier this year, the President had called Gaddafi a 'flaky barbarian' and a 'mad dog', they had complained roundly that this was not the kind of behaviour expected or wanted from the leader of the Western world. When US warplanes had flown over the Gulf of Sidra in defiance of Gaddafi's claim to several score miles of Mediterranean, they had cried foul. 'Needless provocation,' they had said. 'Only make the Colonel bigger than he really is,' they had said. Now, suddenly, as if they had just seen a ghost, they turned pale and said they were 'deeply troubled', that the raid played on so many emotions at once that they were having difficulty deciding how to respond. Were they morally numbed perhaps? Not at all. In place of strongly held views opposing the use of force in, say, Central America, they suddenly wanted to debate when and how a great power like the United States should use force against a festering irritant like Gaddafi. They argued, many for the first time, that a prudent critic of the administration should, every so often, hold off. That way he or she becomes more credible.

Why did they choose this moment to be silent? What happened? Whenever a head of state takes bold military action abroad, the citizenry applaud; witness the Falklands and Grenada. But the din over Libya had to be heard to be believed. Many more Americans than ever before, or so it seemed, were ready to cast aside the maxims of law, evidence, morality, self-interest and common sense in favour of a brutish exposition of military power. They believed in it as zealots, even though they knew it was a symbolic gesture, not a cure, and yet they responded as though the very existence of their homeland depended on supporting it. How did Reagan convert terrorism directed at Americans abroad into the functional equivalent of aggression between states, and how did he elevate Gaddafi into the symbol of terrorism?

Terrorism

To talk of Ronald Reagan as a great communicator is correct but misleading, because it glosses over the essential element of his communicating which is, simply, that he lies. The plain fact is that this administration has developed a very accomplished propaganda machine, using all the tools of the trade, such as obfuscating science and classified intelligence to gain acceptance of the lie. Many Americans know this; while they accept that all governments lie, they think that this administration has been particularly sleazy in its manipulation of information, but they are reluctant to discuss it. The reason is that Americans find it deeply troubling to have to admit that their open system of government, with its almost endless access to official information, and its much-admired Freedom of Information Act, should also permit such widespread corruption of information.

Good propaganda has several layers to it. First, through a variety of media, it builds a case for taking action, military or otherwise, which the government deems necessary. Then it makes the public feel good about what has happened and, finally, in case anything goes awry in the prosecution of the action – the wrong target is hit, there is unacceptable 'collateral damage' or the mission fails altogether – there is a contingency plan to make the public feel good anyway. So it was with Reagan's campaign against Libya.

Since taking office in 1981 the Reagan administration has carried out a protracted, often open debate on whether, as then Secretary of State Alexander Haig put it, to 'cut out the cancer of Gaddafi'. What to do about the Libyan leader and his support of international terrorism has been the subject of endless secret meetings involving Reagan's top national security aides, but also almost as many very public discussions of sanctions, covert actions and the use of military force. The President has involved himself personally in deliberate escalation of a war of nerves between Washington and Tripoli. The war began five months into Reagan's first term, in May 1981, when the US closed the Libyan diplomatic mission in Washington, citing Gaddafi's support for international terrorism. In August that year, Libyan warplanes clashed over the disputed waters of the Gulf of Sidra for the first time and two Libyan jets were shot down. US intelligence reported immediately afterwards that Libyan hit squads were planning reprisals including the assassination of American envoys in Europe – and even assassination of the President himself. The reports prompted Washington first to ban American citizens from travelling to Libya, and then, over the coming months, to make a series of presidential appeals – largely unheeded – for US citizens to leave Libya. In November the Heritage Foundation, the flagwaving current affairs institute of the Reaganite right, called for an oil embargo on Libya to 'take advantage of Gaddafi's weaknesses'. In March 1982, the US banned imports of

Libyan crude oil and curtailed exports of technology to Libya. In 1983, Libya complained that the US was jamming its communications and warned that the Gulf of Sidra would become a bay of 'blood and fire' if US warships entered it. In August that year, US navy jetfighters from the carrier *Eisenhower* intercepted two Libyan MiG-23s off the Libyan coast, but there was no fighting. The MiGs turned away. The following year, 1984, US warplanes from the carrier *Saratoga* again flew provocative flights over the Gulf of Sidra, but without incident.

In 1986, the 'war' escalated rapidly. In January, Reagan ordered American banks to freeze Libyan assets and banned nearly all US trade with Libya, a move which had been considered by the administration five years before but rejected as too drastic. During these five years, Secretary of State George Shultz, the cabinet officer in charge of formulating the US counter-terrorism policy and also the official who has primary responsibility for determining the meaning of terrorism for the executive branch of the US government, began to equate terrorism with war, and to emphasise the rise of what has become known as 'state-sponsored terrorism'. Shultz was supported in his rhetoric by defence secretary Casper Weinberger, who called terrorism 'a new kind of war', and also by Jeanne Kirkpatrick, then US Ambassador to the United Nations. She said with characteristic all-embracing certainty,

> Terrorism is a form of war against society and all who embody it . . . terrorist war is part of a total war which sees the whole of society as the enemy, and all members of a society as appropriate objects for violent action.

Shultz warmed to her theme:

> Terrorism poses a direct threat not only to Western strategic interests but to the very moral principles that undergird Western democratic society. The enemies of the West are united. So too must the democratic countries be united in a common defence against terrorism.

In January this year, Shultz warned that the administration was 'pretty much at the end of the road' on economic sanctions against Libya. Only war would be next.

So many terrorism think-tanks have appeared to mirror the administration's drive that it is possible to get any set of figures you like to fit any hypothesis you may have. Thus the President likes to say that there have been more than 6,550 terrorist incidents over the past decade and approximately 40 per cent of these have been targeted against Americans. However, look at another set of figures and you have 25,000 terrorist incidents reported between 1970-85, and only 5 per cent of these have taken place in the United States. 52 per cent were in Latin America, 25 per cent in Europe and 12 per cent in the Middle East. It is true that more Americans have been killed or wounded in terrorist attacks outside the United States in the past 30 months than in the previous 13 years, but of the 812 incidents of international terrorism in 1985 fewer than 20 involved Americans and a total of 23 Americans were killed – about one fourth the number who die each year as a result of being struck by lightning. In the end the figures are confusing, but Americans have got the message Reagan wanted them to get: terrorism is on the increase.

By the turn of the year, administration officials involved in developing the concept and rhetoric of the new terrorism knew they were playing to the gallery. Although the two major terrorist attacks against the US – the 1983 suicide bombing of the US Marine headquarters in Beirut, in which 241 servicemen lost their lives, and the 1985 hijacking of the TWA flight 847 – were not linked to Libya, violence against American civilians took a dramatic turn. Two further terrorist attacks, aimed specifically against civilians, angered Americans and the President, as never before. In the first, last October, the Italian cruise ship *Achille Lauro* was hijacked and a 69-year-old American tourist in a wheelchair was murdered. In the second, on 27 December, Rome and Vienna airports were attacked and an 11-year-old American girl was among the 15 people killed. US intelligence reported for the first time possession of 'incontrovertible' evidence linking Libya to the airport attacks.

The administration's own studies show that 78 per cent of Americans now consider terrorism to be one of the most serious problems facing the US government – along with the deficit, strategic arms control and unemployment. Americans have also become increasingly fearful, feel more vulnerable, victimised and angry. Even though most Americans still believe that the government is virtually helpless when it comes to catching terrorists, they feel that something should be done. They believe that terrorism reduces America's status in the world and they do not like to be seen, according to Vice-President Bush's February 1986 task force on terrorism report, as pawns – powerless, easily manipulated and at the mercy of the attackers because Americans do not fight back. In response to a task-force questionnaire, Americans complained that there was no cohesive policy on terrorism; they wanted leadership. Reagan was about to give it to them the way he knows best – by swatting gadflies.

Alongside the development of a terrorism cult came efforts to place Gaddafi in the Mad Dictator department. This was easy, given that the subject often obliged by providing his own evidence, and also that the audience was so willing. Apart from Reagan's sustained rhetoric about the Colonel, there was a series of leaked intelligence reports about his 'state of mind'. Intelligence leaks go down very well in America, particularly when they confirm widely held views, such as that the Soviets use chemical and biological warfare, that the Soviets cheat on nuclear arms treaties. Such reports can be an extremely effective instrument of government, and the ones released about Gaddafi were particularly well constructed. They did not say that Gaddafi is crazy, instead they were low key, matter-of-fact reports, that played on all the fears and prejudices of Middle America.

For example, in March 1982, the muckraking syndicated columnist Jack Anderson, a frequent conduit of CIA intelligence leaks, ran a column which began,

> There is a tendency in Washington to refer to the Libyan dictator, Muammar Gaddafi, as a crazy man. Armchair psychologists justify the glib label by pointing to his fanatic extremism, his failure to put realistic limits on boastful pronouncements and his periodic fits of deep depression when he retreats to the desert and broods in his tent.

Americans, cautioned Anderson, should look for more professional analysis. Who should really know about this kind of thing? The Israelis, of course. And Anderson happened to have to hand the latest Israeli intelligence report on Gaddafi – compiled after years of research. The Israelis had concluded that Gaddafi was not 'crazy'. Such labels were not helpful, anyway. But mark the hidden persuaders at work in the next two sentences.

> Among juicier suggestions in the various intelligence reports analyzed by the Israelis was that Gaddafi's behavioural quirks were the result of brain damage from venereal disease. But the [Israeli] profile says this possibility cannot be verified. Apart from mental problems that could be associated with syphilis, there is no evidence that Gaddafi suffers from symptoms matching the disease. There have been reports that Gaddafi suffers from schizophrenia, paranoia, hysteria and serious psychoneurotic disturbances.

However, the profile concludes, 'available evidence is insufficient to confirm or deny whether he has a mental illness'. In other words, Gaddafi *might* be suffering from a host of other mental illnesses. Interestingly, the report did say that Gaddafi had been (then) the leader of Libya for 12 years and:

> It is difficult to believe that a man suffering from maniacal [*sic*] depressive psychoses would be capable of withstanding the pressures that he has been under for such a long time and with such stability without our being witness to repeated outbreaks of illness.

But, in the murky world of intelligence assessments, appraisals of one's enemies can change overnight if the political need arises.

In the immediate aftermath of the raid, Gaddafi was silent for several days. According to a new CIA report, leaked to reporter Bob Woodward of the *Washington Post*, Gaddafi's silence was because he had 'begun displaying the extravagant mood swings of a manic depressive . . . an intelligence source predicted that Gaddafi would soon cycle back [*sic*] into his familiar mould as a wild, outspoken leader, and in all likelihood will begin planning retaliation against the United States. "A lamb one day, and a lion the next", said one well-placed source'. Woodward did not stop there. Gaddafi, according to reliable reports, also used excessive amounts of sleeping pills and stimulants. In late April, *Newsweek* magazine reported that an updated CIA profile said Gaddafi was using hallucinogens, and that one source conferring with him during the Gulf of Sidra exercises found him 'disoriented and incomprehensible'. Finally, in the lead up to the raid, part of the US intelligence community's task was to prepare the American public for the fact that Gaddafi might be killed by US bombs; that the main outcome of the raid might be the assassination of a national leader the United States found undesirable, an act which Congress had outlawed. (A new anti-terrorism bill before Congress would apparently allow the President to order the assassination of anyone who runs a terrorist country.)

In the event, Gaddafi's post-raid silence presented a chance for some of these contingency plans to be revealed. So unpredictable was the result of the bombing thought to be by the administration that they had prefabricated statements in case of Gaddafi's death. It would have been said to be 'fortuitous' and 'serendipitous', but in any case it happened by chance, not design. Had he died, it would, commented Secretary of State George Shultz, have been 'all to the good', but that is not what many Americans think. Having been on the receiving end of assassinations of major public figures, many Americans still think it would have been morally wrong to have killed Gaddafi. In an intensely religious society where the ethics of military action have been an ever-present topic of discussion during this administration, many Americans feel like James Turner Thomson, university ethics professor and author of several books on the ethics of war. He wrote after the raid,

> We don't have to be historians to 'know' inside ourselves that there are right and wrong ways to act, even in the struggle against evil; assassination is wrong, yet military action can be right. For all of America's diversity and individualism it is clear that the underlying fabric which makes us a community still holds, and our beliefs about assassination are part of that fabric.

What, then, if Gaddafi had been killed? The Reagan administration was ready to blame the Russians. On 16 April, the day after the raid, with Gaddafi still 'missing', the administration charged that the Soviet Union was partly to blame for the attack because it had ignored an American request to deter Libyan terrorists from the 5 April bombing of the La Belle nightclub in West Berlin, and because it had supplied Gaddafi with SAM5 anti-aircraft missiles which had encouraged him 'to take risks which would force us to respond'. On the nightclub bombing, the State Department complained,

> On March 27 we advised Soviet officials here and in Berlin that we had evidence indicating Libya was planning actions against the US interests and citizens in Berlin. We urged the Soviets and East Germans to restrain the Libyans. Had they done so, this entire cycle of events would have been avoided.

OPERATION EL DORADO CANYON: GLOBALISING THE COLD WAR

Robin Luckham

Three subjects dominated the agenda of the 1986 Tokyo economic summit: imbalances in the global economy; the Chernobyl nuclear disaster; and 'international terrorism'. The latter had been thrust to the fore, not so much by any upsurge in terrorist activity, as by the United States' bombing raid against Libya, Operation El Dorado Canyon. For President Reagan and Mrs Thatcher the summit was an opportunity to legitimise the US's own state terrorism, and the UK's complicity in it. Indeed, before the summit, both leaders had said they would not exclude military action against Syria and Iran, as well as Libya, if terrorist attacks continued. The other Western powers saw the summit as an exercise in damage limitation, hoping it would heal the split opened up by the US's disregard for the views of its allies. The price Europe and Japan were expected to pay for healing the rift was support for diplomatic sanctions against Libya and tougher measures against terrorism. The price extracted from the US – apart from loss of good will – was less evident.

Asked on British television what he thought of Libya's protestations at the UN Security Council that it opposed terrorism, General Vernon Walters (Mr Reagan's roving envoy) replied, 'that's humpty dumpty language'. The same might also be said of the US administration's own assertion that it had bombed Libya in order to deter terrorism. 'Terrorism' is not so much a definable set of enemies as an abstract word, a series of mirages that tend to recede, when bombed or strafed, into the desert. Like other mirages, everything turns on how and by whom it is perceived. In this there is a certain similarity to the rhetoric of deterrence, constructed around the elaborate mirrored structure of 'threat perceptions'. Both concepts, TERRORISM and DETERRENCE, convey semantic promises of limitless violence. The difference is that deterrence is built around a mutual balance of terror between superpowers or military blocs. Terrorism on the other hand is the violence of the weak against the strong, as defined within semantic space appropriated by the latter – who condemn its methods and refuse to discuss the legitimacy of its goals.

Historically, the term was first used to describe violent acts carried out by individuals and groups against the state. Its present use derives from the processes of decolonisation, national liberation and the imposition upon these struggles of the cognitive frame of the Cold War. Those who use it veer inconsistently between broad and narrow definitions. Broadly constructed, it refers to virtually any use of violence against the civilian population by individuals and groups for political ends. In practice the judgements about which particular uses of violence are considered terrorism have normally been made on ideological grounds. Whether or not Sandinista guerrillas or Contras, Irgun or PLO, SWAPO or UNITA were or are regarded as terrorists or freedom fighters, has been a question of political judgement. From decolonisation, the decisive criterion for the Western powers has always been whether or not the groups in question are to be regarded as serious threats to the established international order and the framework of global capitalism. This is, moreover, a criterion which has acquired institutional roots in the West's own military establishments through the doctrine and practice of 'counter-revolutionary war' and 'counter-insurgency'.

In a narrower use, however, *international* terrorism refers to violence directed specifically against the global infrastructure: communications, air and sea transport, and the West's own international network of bases and military facilities, through which its hegemony is orchestrated. It is an alleged increase in this form of terrorism which provided the occasion for the US assault on Libya. Not only has the number of terrorist attacks, as defined and measured by the Pentagon, been on the increase, but these attacks have become increasingly lethal, claiming larger numbers of victims.

Yet the scale of these terrorist attacks and the casualties they have caused (with probably no more that one or two thousand fatalities annually) pales into insignificance beside the damage inflicted by four decades of permanent armed conflict in the Third World. Major difficulties surround estimation of the spread of war and of its human and material costs. But about broad trends there is little dispute. More wars have occurred since World War II and more people have been killed in them than in any period in history except the two world wars themselves. In *World Military and Social Expenditures*, Ruth Sivard estimates that some 120 wars involving more than a thousand casualties have taken place since 1945, bringing in their train 19 million or so deaths, more than 60 per cent of them civilians. The authors of *The War Atlas* estimate no less than 277 wars between 1945 and 1982, all but 18 in the developing regions. Fifteen of these were major wars between states, 62 were border conflicts and the remainder (200, or 72 per cent of the total) were internal civil conflicts. A clear majority of these conflicts have been exacerbated by one or another form of outside intervention, varying from covert and limited logistical support to full participation in large-scale wars as in Vietnam or Afghanistan. To these must be added the silent emergencies of poverty, famine and disease brought on by drought and other natural disasters (see table below), but often made much worse by armed conflict and political instability.

As the figures indicate, the risks of war are increasingly borne by civilians, the vast majority of them in the Third World. In World War I only around 11 per cent of casualties were civilians; by World War II the proportion had risen to 53 per cent. In the wars of the 1960s, 1970s and 1980s it was 52, 68 and 76 per cent respectively. The new generations of conventional weapons, such as cluster and fragmentation bombs, napalm and fuel-air explosives, can cause indiscriminate damage across far wider areas than earlier munitions. Devastation is increased by the use of techniques of economic denial, including destruction of crops and human settlements and economic blockades. In addition, many conflicts are not conventional wars between states, being rooted in much broader social contradictions and upheavals, and sharpened by external intervention.

Most major emergencies affect many more people than those whose deaths they cause directly, as can be seen in the table. So do war and armed conflict. Yet there are no estimates that are even remotely reliable. One major consequence of any war situation is the displacement of large numbers of persons from their homes, employment and livelihood. There are currently some 11 million refugees worldwide, the great majority (approximately 9 million) migrating from and finding refuge in the developing countries. In addition, it is impossible to guess how many millions have been displaced within their own countries.

Human costs of war and other emergencies

Type of Event	*Number Dying Per Year (Thousands)*		*Number of People Affected Per Year (Thousands)*	
	1960s	1970s	1960s	1970s
Drought	1	23	18,500	24,000
Flood	2	5	5,200	15,400
Tropical Cyclones	11	34	2,500	2,800
Earthquakes	5	39	200	1,200
Others*	6	42	1,300	4,500
Total Disasters	23	143	27,700	48,300
Deaths in Wars	439	587	–	–
Civilians as Percentage of War Dead	52%	68%	–	–

Note: * includes some victims of civil strife and conflict

Sources: Disaster casualties are Red Cross figures presented in Anders Wijkman and Lloyd Timberlake, *Natural Disasters: Acts of God or Acts of Man*? (London: Earthscan, 1984). War deaths are from Ruth L. Sivard, *World Military and Social Expenditures, 1985*.

Why, against such a background, is international terrorism placed at the forefront of the international agenda, meriting a full-scale military attack on Libya by the United States and discussion at the Western summit? One reason would seem to be that for the first time significant numbers of Westerners are directly experiencing the risk and inconvenience of the wars and struggles that have hitherto been waged for them by proxy in the Third World. Large numbers of people are obliged to consider the risks of international travel. These risks may be no higher than those of being mugged in a major city such as New York.

But what is crucial is that they break the carefully constructed quarantine between unstable Cold War peace in Europe and North America and permanent armed conflict fuelled by the arms race in the Third World.

The hysteria and racism of Western statements about terrorism, fundamentalist Islam, Libya and Gaddafi described by other contributors to this book fit with this explanation. Yet there have been other reasons behind the American attack. A hint of what these are is to be found in the revival by Western leaders of the concept of state terrorism. As the US Secretary of State for Defence, Casper Weinberger, put it recently, terrorism has increasingly become a 'state-practised activity, a method of waging war' planned and organised by governments. As such, it can in principle be deterred by the use of force against states which lend it their support. To quote the US Secretary of State, George Shultz, 'if you raise the costs [of inciting terrorism], you do something that should eventually act as a deterrent'. This brings terrorism full circle. Originally conceived of as terror against the state, it has been redefined by the Western powers to include acts of state rebellion against the existing international order, which must be punished with the full panoply of the military force at their disposal.

There is no denying that Colonel Gaddafi has consistently opposed Western hegemony, making use of his oil revenues and his strategic position at the confluence of the Arab world, the Mediterranean and Africa. Among other things, he has provided financial aid and logistical support to 'terrorists' (or liberation movements) in the Arab world and elsewhere, for example the IRA. He has supplied arms acquired from the USSR both to liberation movements and to other Arab states. He has provided military and diplomatic support to beleaguered African governments (not all of which – most notoriously the government of Idi Amin in Uganda – were deserving). He has intervened with his own troops in the protracted struggle for power in Chad.

Yet he has suffered defeats as well as victories, being forced into a military stalemate by France and the US in Chad, losing his chairmanship of the Organisation of African Unity in 1982 because of splits over Chad and the Western Sahara, and suffering a major decline in his country's oil revenues after the collapse of the international petroleum market. It is acknowledged by Western governments, including the US administration, that Colonel Gaddafi is not even the most important Arab source of support for terrorism. Rather, it was Libya's vulnerability which laid it open to attack. Nor can it be convincingly argued that the raid was intended to deter other Arab states, notably Syria and Iran. They were not targeted because of the danger of triggering a broader Middle East and possibly global escalation. By the same reasoning, they are unlikely to have been deterred by the attack on Libya.

In a remarkably lucid interview shortly after the bombing, Colonel Gaddafi himself argued that 'there are deep political reasons as well' for the attack. These arise on the one hand from US fears that a combination of political change in the Arab world, 'victory of the Green movement in West Germany and Europe' and Soviet naval deployments in the Mediterranean will exclude them from a presence in the area. The attack not only sought to pre-empt these changes, but also had a broader imperial purpose, being no less than:

> a very dangerous move by the NATO alliance inspired by the United States to destabilise the balance that was worked out after the Second World War. It is an experiment beginning with Libya to upset this balance. They thought they had found the right moment to change the international balance of power (Interview in *Today*, Sunday 27 April 1986).

Operation El Dorado Canyon seems indeed to form part of a broader US project. This project has three main components. First, the revitalisation of geopolitics around the simultaneous pursuit of the new Cold War and recovery from recession. Second, the development of new strategies and weapons systems (such as the SDI, Air Land Battle and the Rapid Deployment Force) which would enable the US and its allies to shatter the Cold War stalemate and attain strategic superiority in Europe and in the Third World. And third, the restructuring of the North Atlantic alliance so that it can accommodate these changes without falling asunder.

Geopolitics and the revaluation of global real estate

The US's confrontation with Libya began, it will be recalled, when the US Navy crossed the so-called 'line of death' in the Gulf of Sidra, in order to establish, as in earlier episodes in 1981 and 1983, its right to navigate this corner of the Mediterranean. For while in Europe the arms race is measured mainly in balances of weapons, in the Third World it is still control of resources, sea lanes and client states that counts. There is a fetishism of territory rather than of armaments. Hence the most distinctive feature of the new Cold War in the Third World has been the revival of geopolitics, reminiscent of an earlier age of imperialism and closely related to the structure of Western economic and political interests.

Another way of putting it is that global strategic real estate is being systematically revalued. This can be readily verified from documents supporting the military budget requests of the major Western powers. The annual reports of the US Secretary of State for Defence and the Military Posture Statements of the US Joint Chiefs-of-Staff in particular have regularly given one-quarter to one-third of their attention to Third World security problems. The Financial Year 1982 Posture Statement of the US Chiefs of Staff starts (on its second page) with a map of oil fields and transport routes, and follows this up with an inventory of US dependence on strategic minerals produced in the Third World. The Posture Statement for 1985 presents a diagram (also on the second page) of potential sources of conflict located in 'resource-rich regions of instability': South-East Asia, Central America, Southern Africa and 'the area stretching from Libya to Afghanistan'.

This revival of geopolitics reflects not merely the prolonging of East/West conflict but also a restructuring of North/South relations. In a time of economic recession, the structures of strategic, of political and of economic risk have become increasingly interconnected. The situation has been exacerbated by the breakdown since the early 1970s of the established system of international economic management (Bretton Woods), which was based upon fixed exchange rates between the major world currencies and upon the supremacy of the dollar. Following this breakdown, international relations could no longer be managed through the dull compulsions of the market. Instead they were in effect restructured through the new Cold War. As the dollar declined, US imperialism was revitalised. Even when the dollar was temporarily restored (in the mid-1980s), it was in the context of major increases in military spending (stimulating demand in the US economy), substantial trade deficits and consequently high interest rates. European governments were prepared under protest to tolerate the imbalance, in order to preserve the Atlantic alliance and avoid a major economic breakdown. The Third World, however, was left with little choice.

Economic restructuring, moreover, was closely allied to a crisis in accumulation within the advanced industrial countries. One major feature of this crisis was a decline in the rate of profit. More important was that such profits as were still to be made came increasingly from speculative activity, rather than from investment in productive capacity, from finance rather than industrial capital. Speculative gains could be made through the manipulation of exchange rates; through takeover bids and the financial restructuring of companies and countries; through bank lending and high interest rates charged on Third World debts; from rents accruing to governments and oil firms entrenched on oil-bearing land; from the 'non-tariff barriers' by which powerful industrial countries protect their markets from imports of cheap manufactures from the newly industrialising countries (NICs); and through the sale of political technologies (weapons, communications equipment and 'white-elephant' industrial projects) to Third World governments.

These speculative gains have been extremely volatile, enhancing the element of risk in international economic relations. They have also been *political* to the extent that they have depended upon the capacity of powerful governments like that of the United States to influence interest and international exchange rates, to restrict trade, to control the supply of technology and armaments and to influence the level of global demand through military spending and budget deficits. Terrorism has made its own distinctive contribution to this overall calculus of risk, since it strikes at the infrastructure of communications and business travel on which the operations of international capital depend.

The strategic value attached to the Third World has thus increased in a complex interaction between rises in natural resource rents, changes in the spread of economic risk, and military and political considerations. For Libya, as for much of the Middle East, the dominant consideration, at least until the collapse of petroleum prices, was the increased rentals accruing to its oil-bearing land during the 1970s: partly stemming from changes in energy demand, partly from Libya's own assertion of sovereignty over its natural resources and partly from the OPEC cartel. Some of the surplus thereby generated was reinvested in weapons – most of them, in Libya's case, from France, Italy and the USSR which became the country's major supplier in the latter part of the 1970s.

For their part, the Western powers sought to reappropriate a share of these rents and of the gains in sovereignty that had been purchased in the form of weapons. The Carter Doctrine of 1980, under which the former President of the United States proclaimed that

> any attempt by any outside force to gain control of the Persian Gulf region will be regarded as an assault on the vital interests of the United States of America and such assault will be repelled by any means necessary, including military force

represented, in the words of his National Security Adviser, Zbigniew Brzezinski,

> a formal recognition of a centrally important reality: that America's security had become interdependent with the security of three central and interrelated strategic zones consisting of Western Europe, the Far East, and the Middle East/Persian Gulf area.

No clearer statement could be made of the relation between the revaluation of oil-bearing lands in the Middle East and the broader purposes of American power. Note, however, that the security framework thus imposed upon the Middle East and Gulf was further consolidated under the Reagan administration's Reagan Doctrine, in spite of a *decline* in oil rents in the first part of the 1980s, and although few serious strategic analysts believed that the US's Rapid Deployment Forces (RDF) could actually protect oil installations in a crisis, or rescue the governments of regional allies.

North Africa is crucial in this security framework because of its proximity to the main air and sea transport routes through to the Middle East, to the Mediterranean and to Europe. Since the Camp David agreement, Egypt has been the lynchpin of the US-sponsored 'peace process' in the Middle East. The US maintains close military relations with Egypt, Morocco and Tunisia; and it has signed agreements with the two former countries to acquire the use of airfields and other military facilities for the RDF. It has more distant but cordial relations with Algeria, where it operates a small military training and arms sales programme. Only Libya has remained consistently hostile to the construction of the US's new security framework.

Military imperatives: towards a global battlefield

Operation El Dorado Canyon was a graphic demonstration of how far the US has proceeded along the road to creating a global warfighting strategy with common forces, equipment, facilities and plans, interconnecting the infrastructures of Third World intervention and of European defence. In it, three different strands of strategic doctrine seemed to intersect.

Firstly, the use of F-111 bombers based in Britain to carry out precision bombing of Libyan targets was made possible by developments in high technology weaponry and in strategic theory which were the logical outcome of the doctrine of 'flexible response'. The most recent manifestation of the latter is the concept of AirLand Battle which has been widely debated in NATO. AirLand Battle appears in two rather different formulations. First, there is the futuristic doctrine developed by the US Army, known as AirLand Battle 2000, which emphasises the assimilation of 'emerging technology' (ET) weapons within existing NATO defences. It also explicitly considers that 'the security interests of the Alliance are affected by events outside the boundaries of NATO' because of the increased energy and resource requirements of the industrialised countries. Secondly, a different version of AirLand Battle was made the basis of tactical doctrine in the 1982 edition of the US Army Field Manual, in which rapid manoeuvre (rather than firepower and linear warfare), deep attack and an integrated (nuclear and non-nuclear) battlefield were the organising concepts. These doctrines have never been considered exclusively relevant to the European theatre. The US Army Field Manual itself states that 'the AirLand Battle doctrine is suited to that which we face not only in Central Europe, but in Korea, Southwest Asia and other contingency areas throughout the world'.

The concept of an integrated battlefield cutting across the threshold between nuclear and conventional war has also been transferred to Third World contingencies. Many of the weapons systems already in use by the US Central Command and other Western intervention forces are dual-capable; as are the sea-launched cruise missiles now being deployed in all the world's major navies. Although both versions of AirLand Battle are officially US rather than NATO doctrine – having been specifically disowned by a number of European members of the alliance – some of their assumptions are already embodied in NATO force planning and are being incorporated in the alliance's new 'Conceptual Military Framework'.

Secondly, there are the doctrines and technologies associated with 'rapid deployment' in Third World emergencies. Units of the rapid deployment force – created in 1980 and renamed US Central Command (USCENTCOM) in 1983, with command responsibility for the Persian Gulf and Middle East – did not participate in the bid against Libya. However, aircraft carrier groups, which are the main naval component of the US's global intervention forces, were prominent in the attack. USCENTCOM is a large military structure of around a quarter of a million men. For the most part it regroups already functioning military units, including four army divisions (two of them air mobile and one mechanised), an air cavalry brigade, marine amphibious forces, seven tactical fighter wings, two strategic bomber squadrons, three carrier battle groups, a naval surface action group and five marine air patrol squadrons. Although specifically assigned to USCENTCOM, these forces can be used in other emergencies – as in the invasion of Grenada. Only a small portion of these (a small headquarters and a carrier battle group) are actually deployed near the Persian Gulf. The US maintains much larger permanent deployments in the Pacific and in the Eastern Mediterranean, some of which are reassignable to USCENTCOM in emergency. In addition the US has undertaken an expansion and reorganisation of its Special Operations Forces – its anti-terrorist, intelligence and unconventional warfare units – under a new Joint Special Operations Agency, established in 1984. The build-up of US intervention forces is backed by a large increase in long-range airlift capability and major new naval deployments. The latter involve the creation of 15 aircraft carrier battle groups and four battleship surface action groups, the latter based on recommissioned World War II battleships armed with Tomahawk long-range cruise missiles.

Thirdly, the US attack on Libya was in direct lineal descent from 'counter-insurgency' strategies put into practice by the US in the battlefields of Vietnam and North America and by Israel in the Middle East. In theory, counter-insurgency is based on good intelligence, socio-economic reform and low intensity combat. In practice, the US has almost invariably fought capital intensive wars in the Third World, with scant regard paid to the political aspirations of the local population or to the casualties inflicted upon them. But it is Israel, above all, which has pioneered the use of so-called 'surgical' strikes against terrorism, as in the Entebbe raid of 1976, in the 1982 invasion of the Lebanon and in last year's bombing of the PLO headquarters in Tunisia.

What links all three of the above deployments in warfighting strategy is that they have created supplementary 'missions' for the conventional military forces of the US and other Western powers; and have legitimised their procurement of new weapon systems. In this manner they have supplemented and in some respects replaced arms exports, through which earlier structural crises of the arms industry had been resolved. Because the greater part of the major powers' own conventional arsenals are locked up in the Cold War stalemate in Europe, warfare outside the NATO area is almost the only way of testing the effectiveness or use-value of these weapons. This was demonstrated with special clarity not only in Libya but also during the Falklands/Malvinas episode, which was regarded by the strategic community as a vital test of the doctrine and practice of high-technology war; and by the arms manufacturers as a useful adjunct to their advertising campaigns. Thus the Third World, it may be argued, is becoming territorial space for the realisation of the value of global arms production.

The NATO connection

The bombing of Libya precipitated an immediate crisis in the Atlantic alliance, assessed by Lord Carrington, NATO's Secretary-General, as being as serious as any he could remember. The US clearly hoped that by its unilateral action it could cajole Europe into supporting it not only against terrorism, but also in its broader policy of constructing a security framework in the Middle East. Hence the importance attached to securing British assent to the use of the F-111s based in the UK – whether or not their participation was militarily essential – and its anger over the refusal of France and Spain to allow the task force to fly over their territory. As for the Europeans, they were apprehensive about two things. First, that the raid would make them more rather than less vulnerable to terrorist attack. Second, that it might create a precedent for the further use of weapons and troops committed to NATO outside the geographical boundaries of the alliance. Thus Lord Carrington lost no time in emphasising that the alliance could not get involved in counter-terrorist action outside Europe, as the limitations on NATO's theatre of operations 'are set in cement'.

In reality, however, NATO has always functioned as both a regional – North Atlantic and European – alliance and as a global arrangement among the major capitalist military powers. When the alliance was created in 1949, it was formally restricted to the North Atlantic area. This was in part because the US was unwilling to commit itself (at least not openly) to supporting the colonial wars then being fought by its European partners. Since Vietnam, on the other hand, it is the Europeans who have been unwilling to commit themselves to the imperial ventures of the United States. Nevertheless, there has developed an informal division of labour among the members of the alliance based largely on bilateral co-operation between its individual members. European members of the alliance maintain major arms sales programmes which compete commercially with those of the United States, but complement the latter politically to the extent that they exclude socialist supplies from Third World military markets. Europe has its own intervention forces – although France and the UK are the only European members of the western alliance with any real pretensions to be able to 'project power' on a global scale.

France in particular has built up its *Forces d'Action Rapide* with 47,000 men at their disposal and a dual role as a nuclear capable mobile force in Europe and as a rapid deployment force in the Third World. Indeed it is these units which France has used since 1983 (with a certain amount of US logistical and intelligence support) to contain Libyan-backed forces in Chad; this being only the most recent in a whole string of interventions in sub-Saharan Africa stretching back over the entire post-colonial period. French and Belgian paratroops, combined with military units from Morocco and French-speaking African states, helped (with US logistical support) to put down the 1978 rebellion in the Shaba province of Zaire; and French-trained Zairean paratroops have in turn operated alongside French troops in Chad.

Since its withdrawal from east of Suez, the UK has played a less visible military role in the Third World than France, with fewer bases outside the NATO area and until recently no formally constituted intervention force. Nevertheless, British troops have continued to be stationed outside the NATO area (in Belize, Hong Kong, the Falklands, etc). The Marines and Paratroop Regiments are organised and trained to operate both within and outside the NATO area. British military teams have been supplied on contract to Third World governments to train their troops and in some cases (notably Oman) to organise actual military operations. And British naval forces have been despatched to 'show the flag' in the Indian Ocean and the Pacific. The 1982 Falklands/Malvinas War demonstrated decisively that Britain was still capable of fighting limited wars in the Third World, as well as rescuing the navy from budget cuts.

Intervention forces are deployed on a unilateral basis by individual Western powers; and are not formally covered by the NATO command structure. Yet there has been much discussion within NATO's consultative bodies, in particular the North Atlantic Assembly, of the need for co-ordination in 'out of area' contingencies. The United States in particular has pressed its allies to take a more active role in policing the Third World. As the FY1986 Annual Report of the US Secretary of Defence puts it in relation to South-West Asia (i.e., the Middle East, the Gulf, and Indian Ocean):

> Many of our friends and allies have long experience – and in some cases still maintain a presence in SWA. France, for example, has naval and tactical air facilities in Djibouti: that could keep the Bab el Mandeb strait open in a conflict. Similarly, the United Kingdom has provided military personnel to assist the Sultan of Oman's military forces and has made arrangements for our using and improving its facilities in Diego Garcia. France, Italy, the United Kingdom, the Netherlands and Norway have all participated in multinational peacekeeping forces in the Middle East. A number of the European allies have provided en route support to US forces deploying to SWA for exercises or other missions. Furthermore, the United Kingdom and France routinely deploy forces to the region. Depending on the situation, external allied support and cooperation could be very helpful to us in a crisis. We and our NATO allies are studying ways for them to compensate in Europe for any diversion of NATO-oriented US forces to SWA in the event of simultaneous conflicts in the two regions.

Nevertheless, this co-operation has never been automatic. The Libyan episode was not the first time European members of the alliance had denied the US use of their facilities and airspace for operations in the Middle East (some did, for example, during the 1973 Arab-Israel war). Moreover it brought to a head contradictions that were already beginning to shake the alliance's foundations. These contradictions have been deepened by what some have called the US's global unilateralism – its pursuit of its global interests on the assumption that it can count on the uncritical backing of its allies. At the same time, they have been fuelled by increasing doubts within Europe itself, both about NATO's capacity to preserve the peace and about its becoming hostage to US policies outside the NATO area. There are evident dangers in this situation, especially if it encourages the US to move still further in the direction of Fortress America. But it also opens up opportunities: both to start de-aligning Europe from NATO and the system of blocs; and to construct relations within the Third World that are not based upon the politics of Rambo and Operation El Dorado Canyon.

LIBYA AND NATO'S OUT-OF-AREA ROLE

Ben Lowe

The area covered by the North Atlantic Treaty Organisation (NATO) is officially confined to mainland United States, the Atlantic to the north of the Tropic of Cancer, Western Europe and the Mediterranean. Libya is outside the NATO area. Yet the American attack on 15 April 1986 may well have been part of a move to extend the NATO area by stealth and to co-ordinate the policy of the Atlantic alliance in the Middle East, the Gulf and North Africa.

In his State of the Union address for 1985, President Reagan proclaimed what is known as the Reagan Doctrine, with its emphasis on 'rolling back' radical Third World regimes and preparing the way for their replacement by pro-Western forces. Now it seems that the United States is trying to solicit allied support for a more belligerently interventionist foreign policy outside the NATO area – even to the point of providing bases in Europe and other facilities.

This chapter provides a background to these developments inside NATO, and puts the events in Libya into that context. It is clear that there are tensions inside the Atlantic alliance over an 'out of area' policy, but even Europeans who opposed the US action may be shifting towards the US position.

In the beginning

When NATO was formed in 1949, many European nations were global powers with colonies widely dispersed around the world. The United States was relatively new to the global policing role, and still faced a large and vocal isolationist constituency at home, as well as a tradition of anti-colonialism. It was the United States that insisted on restricting the NATO area to exclude Africa and the Middle East, despite European wishes. Thus, the Tropic of

Cancer became the southernmost boundary, and only Algeria in North Africa was included in the NATO area, because France insisted on its inclusion while it remained a French department.

From the outset, it was agreed that NATO members would make their own decisions on how to deal with military developments outside the NATO area. There was to be discussion in the alliance on general Western policy towards the Third World; NATO members fighting wars in the Third World might expect to receive various kinds of support from their allies; and there were regular statements in NATO communiques regarding the importance of monitoring developments in the Third World. But collective military operations outside the NATO area were ruled out.

The first sign of a change in this position came in 1973. It may be that the US felt the need to institutionalise alliance support because the allies were no longer individually reliable. In the 1973 Arab–Israeli war, several European countries refused to provide logistical support for the US airlift to Israel. NATO agreed that planning for operations outside the NATO area could take place at the headquarters of the Atlantic Command (NATO's Navy) at Norfolk, Virginia. This was also the headquarters of the US Navy's Middle East force. But it was the revolution in Iran in 1979, and the Soviet invasion of Afghanistan which prompted a much more significant development. The decision to create a Rapid Deployment Force, primarily in order to intervene in the Gulf area, required concerted action by the NATO alliance. If nothing else, the US needed Western European powers to provide assistance to its interventionist forces, and to compensate for their absence from NATO territory.

The RDF and NATO

The Rapid Deployment Force was created early in 1980 following a decision at the highest levels of the Carter administration. Originally, it was allocated some 220,000 troops, but this was due to double by 1989. Most of these troops are based in the United States, but some forces are with America's Sixth and Seventh Fleets, and some potential RDF units are based in Europe. In 1983, a Central Command was created, to cover 19 states from the Horn of Africa, through the Middle East and up to Pakistan and Afghanistan. This is the main area for RDF activity, although RDF units can well be sent elsewhere and did indeed play a central role in America's invasion of Grenada.

As soon as the RDF was created, there was pressure on NATO allies to join the initiative, in particular by committing their own interventionist forces. However, the reaction was generally cool, largely because, as defence correspondent Luigi Caligaris has written, it appeared 'politically unattractive, militarily inappropriate, and economically far too costly'. The initial coolness of the European reaction did not deter the Americans. They sought European assistance in two specific forms: firstly, to ensure that RDF forces in the US could reach their destination in the Gulf or elsewhere, and to secure European substitute forces for NATO to replace those lost; secondly, to encourage the French, British and Italian governments to provide modest interventionist forces to back up the Americans. The West German foreign minister, Genscher, summed up the broad approach adopted:

> There are common interests in this matter, but not all members are equally fit to the same task. There are members that because of their tradition, history and engagement are more fit than the Federal Republic to safeguard the [area outside NATO] . . . It is a joint co-ordinated strategy that is involved, where every partner will take on the task he is best suited for. Division of labour is necessary.

The role of countries such as West Germany in this division of labour was to assist with transport of troops and to supply the reserve forces for NATO. Transport help was needed to get large numbers of forces from the US mainland, via Western Europe, to the RDF area. Thus bases had to be modified, ammunition dumps created, and supplies stored. All this was provided under so-called Wartime Host Nation Support agreements, in which Britain also participated.

The other aspect of these support agreements was the provision of reserves. This was required because many of the US forces allocated to the RDF were previously allocated to NATO.

The creation of the interventionist force consequently meant that NATO was potentially short of up to 100,000 troops in the event of a major crisis or war – especially if there were a simultaneous crisis in South-West Asia. West Germany and one or two other Allies agreed to make up part of this potential deficiency through the creation of additional reserve forces.

The allies capable of offering their own interventionist forces – Britain, France and Italy – have helped in a variety of ways. Britain has for some time been developing its own Rapid Deployment Force, some 10,000 strong and comprising two units of roughly equal size. It also has such units as the SAS and the Special Boat Squadron. Moreover, Britain has provided the Americans with huge rent-free real estate in the Indian Ocean, in the form of the archipelago of Diego Garcia, for use as a main overseas staging post for their Rapid Deployment Force. This assistance has been described in *NATO Review* as 'the kind of alliance within an alliance which carries benefits for both parties and for NATO as a whole'.

France has a larger fleet in the Indian Ocean than any other NATO member, and has forces and bases in North Africa that could play a role in interventions in the Third World. It also has a 50,000 strong 'Rapid Action Force' for use in either Europe or the Third World. In the 1970s, France was dubbed the 'gendarme otanisé' (OTAN is NATO in French) for its role in intervening of behalf of the West in Zaire, and had been the NATO power willing to engage Libyan forces prior to the recent US attack. Its forces took on Libyan-backed forces in Chad in 1983 in an operation welcomed in NATO circles, and France bombed Libyan-built airfields in northern Chad shortly before the recent US attack on Libya.

Italy's intervention capabilities are limited. The initial decision to create a special force was taken in 1981, but progress was slow. When a further decision was taken, in 1985, to proceed rapidly with the creation of a tri-service interventionist force for use in the Mediterranean area in general, much had already been learned from Italy's first tenative involvement in a NATO 'out of area' force in the Lebanon in 1983. The Lebanon operation by US, British, French and Italian forces came in the wake of the Israeli invasion and eventual withdrawal from Beirut. The idea was to project this force as a 'multilateral peacekeeping force', and within NATO it was emphasised that it should not be seen as a 'collective military action'. However, there are reasons to believe that this joint force was to pave the way for a series of similar operations, in which NATO forces could act together outside the NATO area without unduly upsetting those who believe it should confine itself to the defence of that area. The first evidence of this is that the peacekeeping force was an all-NATO operation in a situation in which the United Nations would normally have been expected to provide a peacekeeping force. A previous exercise, in the Sinai, used NATO and other forces; this was the first purely NATO operation of this kind. Secondly, the exercise involved Italy for the first time in a new out-of-area role together with Britain, France and the US.

From the point of view of the US attack on Libya, it was significant that the operation in the Lebanon ended in disaster. For, following the bomb blasts that killed 236 Americans and many French, the notion of a 'peacekeeping' approach to Western interests in the Middle East died a rapid death. The hawks who advocated a much more belligerent interventionist strategy began to gain the ascendancy in Washington. This was to have implications for NATO, for Central America, and above all for Libya.

'Terrorism' as a Third World War

One immediate response to the loss of so many of its servicemen in Beirut was the US invasion of Grenada. This seemed to indicate that America's interventionist policy in the Third World had moved up a gear and that direct military intervention was now possible in other countries, not least Nicaragua. What seems to have happened, according to the *New York Times*, is that the US administration opted to

> improve its ability to use *specialized forms of force* in situations in which the open exercise of power and the deployment of large numbers of men and weapons would be politically unacceptable.

In 1983, America was still living under the shadow of the

Vietnam War in two important respects: the loss of US personnel in the defence of overseas interests was still a very sensitive political issue which no interventionist policy could ignore; and America's capacity to use 'specialised forms of force' – sabotage operations, psychological warfare techniques, etc – had been much impaired, not least by the exposés of CIA malpractice during the 1970s. In the late 1970s, urgent efforts were made to overcome this 'Vietnam syndrome', through whipping up anti-Soviet feeling. Reagan rode this bandwagon, with his rhetoric of the 'evil empire', and the new Cold War had begun.

However, there has been a tendency in recent years to label the main threat to the United States 'terrorism'. At its most extreme, this 'anti-terrorist' camp has talked of the 'Third World War' having already begun, and has argued that this war entails 'brush-fire conflicts, assassinations, terrorist bombings, coups, revolutions, and civil strife, most of it concentrated in the Third World'. The anti-terrorist cause has reached a level of mania comparable to earlier waves of anti-communism. As such it has influenced White House policy, prompted the creation of new (and sometimes secret) forces, and altered the assumptions underlying debates in the US Congress.

The US policy on 'terrorism' and radical Third World governments has recently gained a level of coherence is what is called the 'Reagan Doctrine'. This entails support for 'contra' forces seeking to overthrow or otherwise weaken the governments of Nicaragua, Angola, Kampuchea, Laos and Afghanistan, and to remove such regimes as Colonel Gaddafi's in Libya. Its catchword is 'the wind of freedom', and it seeks to draw a parallel between popular forces against dictatorship in, for instance, the Phillippines and the 'contra' forces it openly backs elsewhere.

The Reagan Doctrine was effectively the inspiration behind the attack on Libya. Whatever its apparent coherence, it was reached through a haphazard process guided by the active 'anti-terrorist' and roll-back lobby. The backing for 'contra' forces did not arise from a general plan. The CIA gradually developed the policy as opportunities arose in different countries. It was not until June 1985 that 'contra' leaders met to discuss their activities. This meeting was in Angola (following an initial gathering in South Africa), where contras from Nicaragua, Angola,

Afghanistan and Laos tried to form what they called a 'Democratic International'. The meeting was organised by multi-millionaire Lewis Lehrman, a close friend of Reagan, who later said 'their goals are our goals'. A year before, a Pentagon official said, 'We're getting involved in insurgency now – rather than what we did in the sixties, which was mainly counter-insurgency. Socialism is not irreversible.'

The units and weapons that America uses in these operations have also emerged from the anti-terrorist and roll-back crusade. Traditional covert forces are used, such as the Special Forces (the Green Berets) and the CIA, but with massive funding now available to them, they have recovered from their post-Vietnam setbacks. There are also special anti-terrorist/counter-insurgency units such as the Navy's SEALS and the Delta Force; and the 12 PSYOP (psychological warfare) battalions have also benefited from increased funding and greater freedom of manoeuvre. There is also a special intelligence unit, the Army Intelligence Support Activity, which was set up as a separate source of intelligence from the CIA and to engage in 'anti-terrorist' activities. This is involved in Nicaragua as well as in Europe. These forces meet precisely the needs of 'low-intensity warfare', which is the new codeword in the US military establishment for the implementation of the Reagan doctrine. The US Army has defined low-intensity warfare thus:

> It includes military operations by or against irregular forces, peacekeeping operations, terrorism, counter-terrorism, rescue operations and military assistance under conditions of armed conflict. This form of conflict does *not* include protracted engagement of opposing regular forces . . . [It is the] limited use of power for political purposes.

'Low-intensity warfare' in many ways represents a compromise inside the US military establishment. There are those who have wanted a fully-fledged military operation ever since Reagan came to power; there are those who would support such an operation only if there were a guarantee that US personnel would not be lost; and there are those who want to limit all military operations to the low-intensity level. Given the preferences of the

President and the role of hawkish interventionists like George Shultz and Donald Regan, larger scale military operations were always on the cards. Many have wanted an attack on Nicaragua, but Congress will not give consistent support for the contras let alone a direct US military assault. Various other countries might have provoked an escalation of the East–West conflict, so only one country remained for a 'clean' attack which could unite public opinion, minimise American casualties and give Reagan prestige. This was Libya.

Libya's almost universal unpopularity made an attack on it less likely to lose America friends. Its relationship with Moscow is less than close, and intelligence indicated that a limited attack could be carried out, with little danger of US losses. However, Libya brought the NATO Alliance into the equation. US bases in NATO countries would need to be used by the Sixth Fleet. Intelligence facilities on NATO territory would need to play a role, and the reaction of NATO leaders would have to be borne in mind. A negative European response would cause problems for the alliance, strengthening calls in the US for an American withdrawal from Europe, and neutralist feeling in Europe. But a positive response might persuade Congress to back other moves – in Libya or elsewhere in the Third World.

The Reagan doctrine and NATO

Any new US policy inevitably affects NATO because of the dominant role of the United States in the Alliance. When President Carter established the Rapid Deployment Force, NATO had to make all kinds of accommodations, including the Wartime Host Nation Support Agreements and European interventionist forces.

In the case of the Reagan Doctrine, much will depend on whether the Alliance begins to see a 'terrorist conspiracy', with Moscow at the core and countries like Nicaragua in the plot. It will also be important whether the Alliance applies the principle that 'limited operations' outside the NATO area are best 'left to individual powers acting separately or in concert'. The Libyan attack has given us a number of pointers on this. There is conflicting evidence concerning direct collusion between the French and Americans in Chad prior to this attack. But the fact that the

US supports the Chad government with military aid and other finance, indicates that Washington and Paris see eye-to-eye on the importance of protecting the Government from the pro-Libyan forces in the north. Shortly before the US attack, NATO Secretary-General Lord Carrington effectively gave his blessing to the assault by telling US TV viewers, 'I don't think the US can sit back and allow this sort of terrorism . . . without taking some form of retaliatory action' and he suggested that US retaliation against Libya could elicit 'a very great deal of sympathy' from Europe. This can only have strengthened the resolve to attack four days later.

Britain then played a full role in the attack. It agreed to a NATO exercise at US and NATO bases in Britain to mask the preparations for the attack, including the work involved in loading the F-111s with hundreds of bombs. And then, of course, came approval for the use of the bases. George Younger, the Defence Minister, has insisted that the two main reasons for the green light were 'the greater safety to civilians and servicemen that would result from using the F-111s, and secondly the strong and overwhelming importance to Britain of the alliance with the United States.' It would appear that it is now the policy of the present Government to back US adventurism wherever it occurs, unless it is an invasion of a British Commonwealth island without the Queen's consent. This represents unambiguous support for the use of NATO bases and NATO equipment outside the NATO area regardless of the views of the rest of NATO and of the possible effect on NATO interests as a whole.

It also confirms a view long expressed by the peace movement in Britain that the US/NATO bases here have more to do with the global interests and unilateral policing role of the United States than the East-West conflict, and that they are more likely to endanger the security of British people than to preserve it. There are precedents for this view, including the US intervention in the Lebanon, in 1958, and the use of ammunition from bases in Britain to supply the Israelis in 1973.

According to the *Sunday Times*, Mrs Thatcher's support for the US attack 'gave President Reagan the public support he needed from Europe . . . [there was] a critical need for the United States to be seen to have an ally.' This is no doubt true, and it is all the more galling for that. But there is the question of the other Europeans in NATO, who may think that the whole affair was a minor disaster from NATO's point of view.

Presumably the US hoped to win over Europeans to the view that places Libya as 'state terrorist number one'. They have to some extent succeeded in getting the Europeans to treat Libya as a 'state terrorist regime', to isolate Libya diplomatically and to take a series of measures which will strengthen anti-Libyan sentiment in Western Europe. The Americans now claim that the military action was justified because it was sufficient to bring the NATO Europeans around to their point of view.

The lesson is twofold; first, the US raids have extended the NATO role to that of a global policeman, under the guise of 'countering terrorism' or some other such ideological dressing. This does not involve NATO members on a collective military basis, but there is a collective position, which means that NATO is implicating itself in much broader questions than the 'East-West' confrontation, and the possible consequence of a conflict in the Third World escalating to the level of an East-West conflict.

The second point is that NATO is no shield against a belligerent America. Many liberals and social democrats will argue, at least while Mr Reagan occupies the White House, that European politicians can better control the US by being its allies in NATO. Without NATO, they argue, America would be a far greater danger to the world. Yet the evidence of April 1986 does not seem to confirm this. Instead, we saw a pusillanimous Europe that was unable to prevent the American attack, for all the supposed consultation procedures available. And no sooner was the attack over but the Europeans were giving every impression, from the White House point of view, that it was justified.

Finally, the question must be asked: if there were no NATO, if there were no bases in NATO Europe for the Sixth Fleet, if there were no bases for the F-111s, if there were no US intelligence facilities in Western Europe, and no NATO exercises to use as a cover for the loading of bombs and the flying in of tankers, would the attack on Libya have occurred?

THE LIBYAN CONTEXT

Paul Anderson

On the night of 31 August 1969, troops under the command of a group of young nationalist officers seized control of key installations in Libya while 79-year-old King Idris was visiting the Turkish spa of Bursta. The coup met no serious resistance.

The young officers announced the formation of a Libyan Arab Republic under the control of a Revolutionary Command Council (RCC). The RCC's first communique, broadcast on Tripoli Radio on the day of the coup, stated that it would create 'a revolutionary and undoctrinal socialist state', based on the ethical values of the Koran, which would transform Libya into a 'progressive nation fighting against colonialism'. The new republic would 'carry the flag of Arab nationalism' and attach great importance to 'the unity of all developing countries'.

The RCC assured diplomats that it had no intention of interfering with foreign oil interests and was promptly recognised by governments throughout the world. A week after the coup, Tripoli Radio named 27-year-old Colonel Muammar al Gaddafi as Commander-in-Chief of the armed forces and Chairman of the RCC. It also announced that the RCC had appointed a cabinet (largely composed of civilians) with Mahmoud Sulaiman Maghrebi as Prime Minister.

The cabinet lasted barely three months. In early December 1969, two of its members, Minister of Defence Colonel Adam al Hawaz and Minister of the Interior Colonel Moussa Ahmad, were accused of plotting a coup. The cabinet resigned, to be replaced in January 1970 by one led by Gaddafi himself.

Libya before the coup

The country Gaddafi took over was one that had undergone dramatic political, social and economic change in the previous half century. Between 1913 and 1942, Libya had been an Italian colony. The colonial regime was brutal; Italian settlers (of whom there were 100,000 in 1942 in a total population of 700,000) drove native farmers from the land into the desert. Any resistance was met with draconian oppressive measures. An estimated 80,000 indigenous Libyans were detained in concentration camps by the Italians, and another 20,000 forced to emigrate. From 1942 to 1951, Libya was administered by the British and French. King Idris, a protégé of the British, came to power in 1951 after a 1949 UN resolution had granted the country a nominal independence.

Until the early 1960s Libya was a poor, predominantly agricultural society, economically reliant on aid granted by the US and Britain in return for military bases on Libyan soil. But in the late 1950s massive oil deposits were discovered: and by 1969 Libya was the second largest oil producer in the Arab world. Gross National Product rose 450 per cent between 1962 and 1968.

This was not, however, reflected in a meteoric rise in living standards for most of the Libyan population (which numbered two million by the mid-1960s). The corrupt, pro-Western monarchy was unwilling or unable to get the oil companies to pay even normal rates for the oil they extracted: the oil companies paid less for Libyan oil than for oil from almost every other producer, even though it was of better than average quality and, because of Libya's geographical position, cheap to transport to major customers. Most of the oil revenues the Idris regime did receive went to line the pockets of the already rich.

By the late 1960s, particularly after the 1967 Arab-Israeli war had reawakened popular antipathy to the role of the West in the Arab world, the ageing Libyan monarch's regime began to look increasingly shaky. Widespread anti-government rioting in 1967 was followed by a period of belated and half-hearted administrative and economic reform: but by early 1969 the momentum of reform had slowed almost to a halt in the face of resistance by conservative vested interests. Few observers were particularly surprised by the coup which swept the monarchy aside. Cynics, of whom there are many in the Arab world, suggested that the Americans had at least acquiesced in Gaddafi's coup, fearing that a pro-communist coup was in the offing.

Pan-Arabism and leadership of OPEC

It became clear from the first three months of the new regime's life that its militant Arab nationalist stance was not merely rhetorical. At home, businesses owned by foreigners (except banks and oil companies) were nationalised; Islamic restrictions on dress and alcohol were enforced; and non-Arab doctors, teachers and technicians were replaced by Arabs. Abroad, the regime immediately began to look for allies in the Arab world. One of Gaddafi's first acts was to visit Egyptian President Nasser, whose 1952 coup and pan-Arabist ideology had been Gaddafi's inspiration. Gaddafi offered Nasser his support, Nasser reciprocated, and in late December 1969 arrived in Tripoli to sign a 'close revolutionary alliance' with Gaddafi and Sudanese President Numeiry.

At the same time as searching for stronger links with the Arab world, Gaddafi began to break some of the Idris regime's ties with the West. In December 1969 Libya negotiated the removal of the US airbase at Wheelus Field outside Tripoli and the smaller British bases at Tobruk and El Adem. From January 1970, it turned its attentions to getting a better deal for Libyan oil.

On 20 January 1970, the Libyan Oil Minister, Ezzedine Mabrouk, told representatives of the 21 oil companies operating in the country that negotiations to raise the price of oil must begin at once. A few days later, the Libyan and Algerian governments issued a joint statement demanding immediate increases in oil prices. On 5 February Iraq announced its support for Libya. During that spring, the Libyans demanded massive cuts in production from the largest company operating there, and the Algerians nationalised six oil companies. The oil companies were terrified by this united front. Worse was to come. In July 1970, Algeria unilaterally raised the price of its oil without consulting the oil companies. The Libyans demanded similar price increases, and nationalised oil product distribution to show they meant business. When Shell resisted the price rise, it was made to shut down production completely. By October 1970, all the oil companies operating in Libya had accepted the government's demands. 'We have won back our rights,' proclaimed a jubilant Gaddafi.

The Libyan and Algerian successes prompted other oil producing countries into enthusiasm for oil price increases. The December 1970 meeting of the Organisation of Petroleum Exporting Countries (OPEC) agreed to press for price increases and increases in the tax on oil production in every member country. The oil companies formed a united front to resist OPEC's demands, and attempted to isolate Libya, Iraq and Algeria within OPEC. In February 1971, with negotiations stalemated, OPEC issued an ultimatum, its first ever: unless the oil companies acceded to its demands, OPEC would start an embargo of recalcitrant companies. The companies' opposition collapsed: on 16 February 1971 they signed the Tehran Agreement, increasing oil prices and taxation at a stroke.

The Algerians, Iraqis and Libyans, now joined by the Saudi Arabians, pressed on. The Libyans were given responsibility for negotiating even greater increases in prices. The oil companies gave in under the threat of a complete cut-off of supplies, signing the Tripoli Agreement of April 1971 which gave Libya an increase 60 per cent higher than that obtained by the Tehran Agreement. Further increases were secured by OPEC after the 1973 Arab-Israeli war. The Libyan government's revenue from oil taxation, which stood at $1,295 million in 1970, reached $5,200 million in 1975.

Falling out with the West

If the negotiation of a better price for Libyan oil was the Gaddafi regime's most significant snub to the West in 1970-71, it was by no means the only one. In July 1970, all property of Italians and non-resident Jews was expropriated. Italian Foreign Minister Aldo Moro (later assassinated by the Red Brigades) protested strongly, but the expropriation went ahead, and most of the 13,000-strong Italian community left Libya in summer 1970. In September the same year, Gaddafi broke diplomatic relations with the pro-Western Jordanian regime of King Hussein after fighting between Jordanian troops and Palestinian guerrillas. In December, foreign banks operating in Libya were nationalised and non-Libyan companies banned from operating banking facilities. In July 1971, Libyan diplomatic ties with another pro-Western Arab regime, that of King Hassan of Morocco, were broken after Tripoli gave premature support to an anti-Hassan coup attempt.

Nevertheless, it would be wrong to believe that Gaddafi had by this stage completely antagonised Western governments. Indeed, the virulent anti-communism of his regime was approved by many in power in the West, particularly after a 1971 communist-backed coup against Numeiry in Sudan was foiled with Libyan help. The Libyans, co-operating with British intelligence services, forced a British commercial aircraft carrying two of the coup leaders to land on Libyan soil. The two leaders were handed to the Sudanese government and executed.

By mid-1972, however, Western governmental attitudes had changed. In December 1971, Gaddafi had nationalised the Libyan holdings of British Petroleum (in retaliation, he said, for the British failure to prevent Iran from occupying the Tumb Islands in the Persian Gulf). This was followed by more nationalisations in 1972-73. He further antagonised the British, first by intervening in the 1971-72 dispute between Britain and Malta over British bases there, offering support for the Mintoff government against Britain, and then by declaring in June 1972 that 'We are making war on Great Britain, and if the Irish revolutionaries want to liberate Ireland we will back them to the hilt.' (Whether there was any substance to Gaddafi's claims to be aiding 'Irish revolutionaries' is, however, an open question. The Ministry of Defence in London immediately stated that 'there is no evidence that Libyan arms are getting through for use by the IRA in Northern Ireland'. In 1973, however, a ship loaded with Libyan arms, with Irish republican leader Joe Cahill on board, was seized off the Irish coast – though many commentators believe that the Libyans had not actually sent any arms to the IRA before this shipment. Others argue that the Libyans themselves tipped off the British authorities as a move in their public relations war with Britain. The extent of Libyan aid to the IRA since 1973 is unknown. A cache of arms in boxes marked 'Libyan Armed Forces' was discovered in the Irish Republic in January 1986, but few intelligent observers think the extent of Libyan aid significant, particularly when compared with the resources the IRA receives from US sympathisers and drinking clubs.)

Development and 'cultural revolution'

Meanwhile at home, Gaddafi was consolidating his regime's position. In June 1971, the Arab Socialist Union was announced as the state's sole political party. Oil revenues were poured into reform and development projects, often haphazardly planned and executed. Expenditure on agricultural development grew 900 per cent between 1970 and 1974, and on industrial development plans 600 per cent. A social welfare system, unique in the Arab world, was rapidly constructed. By the mid-1970s, Libyans were enjoying free education and housing, subsidised cars and shops overflowing with imported consumer goods. One of the regime's biggest problems was a shortage of skilled labour; the arrival of oil wealth in an essentially agricultural society did not instantaneously produce a class of skilled industrial and construction workers, let alone one of technicians and managers. Gaddafi's response was to buy in skills. From the early 1970s, thousands of foreign workers (mainly from poor Arab countries but also from Europe) were employed on Libyan projects. In 1975, 42 per cent of the Libyan labour force was of non-Libyan origin.

Unsurprisingly, Gaddafi was popular with most of his subjects, who attributed their new-found prosperity to his regime. Not that they would have had much opportunity to criticise if they had wanted to; heavy censorship was in force, and suspected opponents of the regime were treated harshly (though no more so than in most other countries of the region). In August 1971, King Idris and 107 of his former politicians and bureaucrats were put on trial (many of them *in absentia*) for alleged corruption: Idris was sentenced to death in his absence, and 76 of the 'defendants' were given prison sentences.

Nevertheless, by 1973 Gaddafi was facing some internal problems. The Arab Socialist Union had failed to attract enough members to provide him with the power base he had hoped to create, and there were signs of growing opposition within the RCC to Gaddafi's radical nationalism. Gaddafi responded by going on to the offensive. In April 1973, he called for the launching of a 'cultural revolution to destroy imported ideologies, whether they are Eastern or Western' and for the creation of a society based on the teachings of the Koran. All 'politically sick' individuals were to be purged, and all imported books were to be destroyed (including those propagating atheism and communism). Arms were to be distributed to the 'revolutionary masses' to protect the revolution. The vehicles for this cultural revolution were 'people's committees' of 16-20 people, with powers to dismiss bureaucrats and managers on grounds of political unreliability, laziness or incompetence. By the end of June 1973, the Libyan regime claimed that some 1,800 such committees had been formed.

The declared aim of the cultural revolution was not only to transform Libyan society. In May 1973, Gaddafi declared that his 'Third International Theory', based on the Koran, was the

> path for all peoples of the world who abhor both materialist capitalism and atheist communism. This path is for all the peoples of the world who abhor the dangerous confrontation between the Warsaw and North Atlantic military alliances. . . . It is also for all the people who oppose racist governments which have built their own structure on the ruins of other nations, like the Israelis who have forcibly acquired the lands of the Palestinians and their neighbours. And it is for all those who support the rights of small nations to enjoy their God-given right to independence, such as those numerous nations enslaved by the Soviet government of Russia.

Unification hopes dashed

Gaddafi's immediate foreign policy aim in launching the cultural revolution, though grandiose, was in reality rather less than global. In July 1972 he had reached agreement with President Anwar Sadat of Egypt that Libya and Egypt should merge on 1 September 1973. (This agreement followed the formation in January 1972 of a Federation of Arab Republics, taking in Egypt, Libya and Syria, which in turn had its origins in the alliance of Libya, Egypt and Sudan agreed by Gaddafi, Nasser and Numeiry in December 1969.) Sadat was unenthusiastic about Gaddafi's plans; the Libyan 'cultural revolution' was in part an attempt to mobilise Egyptian public opinion in favour of the merger. In July 1973, Gaddafi announced that a giant convoy of vehicles containing 40,000 Libyans would arrive shortly in Cairo to encourage the merger process. In the event, the 'Green March' on Cairo was a chaotic failure. Sadat was not at all impressed by the prospect of 40,000 Libyans arriving on his doorstep and was not moved even by Gaddafi's histrionic resignation during the Green March (the resignation was later withdrawn). Most Egyptians found the whole episode rather amusing. The Libyans turned back before they reached Cairo. Although Sadat and Gaddafi signed an agreement to merge the two countries in late August 1973, the union was never effective. Sadat's mistrust of Gaddafi had become such that, when Sadat made the decision to go to war with Israel in October 1973, Gaddafi was not told of the decision (let alone consulted). Gaddafi (although an enthusiastic proponent of Arab victory and an important source of arms and money for Sadat) was extremely critical of Sadat's handling of the war, which ended in an ignominious defeat for the Arab side. After the defeat, he refused to attend an emergency Algiers meeting of Arab heads of state, declaring that it would only ratify capitulation. In late 1973, a freeze in Libyan-Egyptian relations began, characterised by mutual accusations of subversive activity and border tensions.

Following the failure of the attempt to unite with Egypt, Gaddafi turned his attentions to Tunisia. On 12 January 1974, after two days of talks, Gaddafi and Tunisian President Bourguiba announced the union of the two countries into an Islamic Arab Republic. But the merger was put on ice when Tunisian Prime Minister Nouira returned from abroad. Gaddafi denounced other Arab leaders for their lack of enthusiasm for pan-Arabism; 'there has been enough chatter about Arab unity by men who run away when the time comes to transform it into reality.'

The revolution continues

The cultural revolution petered out soon after the failure of the Green March. And in April 1974, it was announced that Gaddafi, while remaining head of state and commander-in-chief of the armed forces, had been relieved of political, administrative and ceremonial duties so that he could devote his energies to ideological and mass organisational work. Western observers speculated that he had been effectively deposed after a power struggle, but after five months of withdrawal Gaddafi re-emerged, and it soon became clear that he was still very much in control (though there was a coup attempt against him in July 1975). During 1975, Gaddafi launched a further stage in his revolution with the publication of the *Green Book*. The *Green Book*, which is the 'basic text' of the Libyan regime in the same way that Mao's *Red Book* was the basic text of communist China in the 1960s and early 1970s, lays down the fundamental principles and objectives of the Libyan regime. It is a strange synthesis of Islamic fundamentalism, Third World Marxism, Nasserite pan-Arabist socialism and quasi-anarchist direct democratic theory. It rails against what it sees as the sham democracy of competitive party politics, and describes a non-party model for Libyan democracy. In its pages Gaddafi polemicises on relations between the sexes and announces the intention of abolishing wage labour and private commerce.

In September 1975, a series of nationalisations was announced affecting the motor trade, land and import traders. In November the RCC announced the formation of a 618-member Grand National Congress, later renamed the General People's Congress (GPC) and expanded in membership, of the Arab Socialist Union. The Congress, which held its first meeting in January 1976, was composed of members of the RCC, leaders of the 'people's congresses' and 'popular committees' set up in 1973, and representatives of trade unions and professional bodies. The first meeting endorsed all decisions made by the RCC and resolved that 'political action' could be exercised only through the GPC; non-compliance with the 'people's democratic experiment' would be seen as 'contrary to the people's will' and would be 'relentlessly crushed'. Gaddafi hailed the Congress as marking the beginning of a new form of democracy.

In November 1976, Gaddafi announced plans for further radical constitutional changes. The March 1977 meeting of the GPC abolished the cabinet and the RCC and changed the country's official name to The Socialist People's Libyan Arab Jamahiriya (roughly 'state of the masses'). The RCC was replaced by a General Secretariat of the GPC with Gaddafi as Secretary-General, and the cabinet was replaced by a 26-member General People's Committee. The Libyan leadership hailed the establishment of the Jamahiriya as momentous. Gaddafi's second-in-command,

Abdesselam Jalloud, hitherto Prime Minister, declared that 'For the first time in history, rulers have handed power over to the people'. In reality, power remained very much in the hands of Gaddafi and his immediate circle. Soon after the March 1977 meeting of the GPC, Gaddafi called for the formation of 'revolutionary committees' to galvanise the revolution. In the beginning, these committees (the members of which were carefully vetted) had an essentially propagandist role. But from 1979, their powers were gradually increased. Directly answerable to Gaddafi, they assumed responsibilities for vetting appointments throughout Libyan society, surveillance and policing, dispensing 'revolutionary justice' and (most recently) supervising the means of production.

In March 1979, after the GPC declared that 'the separation of the state from the revolution' and 'the vesting of power in the masses' had been completed. Gaddafi resigned as Secretary-General to concentrate on 'revolutionary work'. The General Secretariat was reorganised and the General People's Committee reduced to 21 members. The Committee was further reduced to 19 members in 1982.

The momentum of the revolution continued unabated until the early 1980s. Workers took over enterprises, proclaiming themselves 'partners and owners'. By 1979, the private sector of the economy (except in agriculture) had shrunk to insignificance. In 1981, in line with the timetable outlined in the *Green Book*, all shops were closed and replaced by huge state supermarkets selling goods at a minimum mark-up.

In late 1979, Gaddafi urged Libyans living abroad to take over Libyan embassies to create 'People's Bureaux'. In early 1980, he issued a call for the 'physical liquidation' of opponents of the revolution living abroad and 'elements obstructing change' at home. An estimated 2,000 people were arrested in the following two months. In April, Gaddafi announced that unless Libyan exiles returned home by 10 June, they would risk the revenge of the revolutionary committees. Since February 1980, several exiled opponents have been assassinated, often by Libyans operating out of People's Bureaux.

How popular these measures were with 'the masses' is difficult to assess. The revolution certainly alienated the small middle class, and many middle-class Libyans (including several one-time members of the regime) had emigrated by the end of the 1970s The *Economist* estimated in 1981 that there were more than 100,000 Libyans in exile). There were also several coup attempts against Gaddafi towards the end of the decade, indicating that at least some sections of the armed forces were unhappy with his rule. But until 1980 oil revenues (and with them living standards) continued to rise, and it seems likely that most poor Libyans gave the regime willing support.

In 1980, however, the price of oil began to fall. Libya's oil revenues dropped from $22,000 million in 1980 to $16,000 million in 1981 and less than $10,000 million in 1982. At first the Gaddafi regime responded to the slump by eating into its substantial reserves, but from 1982 it was forced to impose austerity measures. Imports of consumer goods were cut (with imports of cars, televisions and videos 'temporarily' banned), many development projects were cancelled or trimmed, and foreign skilled workers were sent home. Although the social welfare system survived more or less intact (as did the military budget), many of the luxuries of the oil boom years were no longer available to most Libyans. Many commentators began to ask whether the Gaddafi regime would lose popularity as a result. So far, however, there has been little sign of popular discontent of any significance (though there have been unsuccessful coup attempts).

Gaddafi's foreign adventures

After the failure of the merger with Tunisia, Gaddafi found himself almost without friends among Arab governments. He turned increasingly to supporting opposition in neighbouring pro-Western states as his chosen means of advancing the pan-Arabist and pan-Islamic causes. Since 1974, Gaddafi has been accused of backing attempted coups or popular rebellions in, among others, Sudan, Egypt, Morocco, Chad and Tunisia.

Egypt Relations with Egypt, strained from late 1973, deteriorated almost to the point of war by 1977. Sadat's visit to Israel in November 1977 was vehemently denounced by Tripoli, and in December Gaddafi hosted a summit of Arab states which rejected Sadat's policy of reconciliation with Israel. When Sadat signed the Camp David agreement in March 1979, there were reports of Libyan troop movements along the Egyptian border. Subsequently, Gaddafi walked out of a Baghdad Arab summit meeting, denouncing the half-heartedness of the sanctions against Egypt which other Arab leaders were considering. Libyan-Egyptian relations have remained frozen to this day.

Tunisia Relations with Tunisia have been rather more variable. In 1976, after the Tunisians alleged Libyan involvement in an attempted coup, Tunisian workers were expelled from Libya. There was a dispute between the two countries over offshore rights. When this was resolved in February 1978, Gaddafi proposed a federation of Libya, Tunisia and Algeria. The Tunisians rejected the proposal and once again relations deteriorated. In January 1980, there was a guerrilla raid on the Tunisian mining town of Gafsa, which the Tunisian government blamed on Libya. Gaddafi denied any involvement. The French sent military aid to Tunisia and the French embassy in Tripoli and consulate in Benghazi were burned as a demonstration of Libyan anger at the French intervention. In 1982, however, relations once again improved. Gaddafi visited Tunis and the two countries signed a co-operation agreement. In late 1985 relations again soured after Gaddafi expelled 30,000 Tunisian workers.

Palestine Gaddafi has not been a major actor in Palestinian politics, but his rhetorical militancy on the Palestinian question is such that he has frequently come close to alienating the leadership of the PLO. He has always tended to lend support to extreme groups within the PLO rather than the mainstream Fatah organisation. In 1980, a serious rift developed between Gaddafi and Fatah leader Yasser Arafat, whom Gaddafi accused of having abandoned the armed struggle in favour of diplomacy. The split was patched up in 1981, but in 1982, with the PLO torn by dissension after the débâcle in the Lebanon, Gaddafi backed the pro-Syrian PLO breakaway faction of Abu Mousa. In recent months, however, relations between Libya and the mainstream PLO have improved.

Syria Gaddafi's relations with Syria have not been as good as might have been expected from a superficial reading of the two regimes' politics. Although both have been strong critics of Egypt and of the mainstream of the PLO, and both have supported Iran in the Gulf War (unlike every other Arab regime), Gaddafi has been consistently wary of the Syrian regime's secularism, while the Syrians have mistrusted the Libyan leader's pretensions to leadership of the Arab world. In September 1980, Gaddafi made an offer of unity to Syria; but the Syrians rejected Libyan overtures.

Chad and sub-Saharan Africa The story of Libyan involvement in Chad is complex. Chad gained independence from France in 1960, and was ruled by N'Garta Tombalbaye from independence until 1975, when he was ousted by a coup. From 1965, the Tombalbaye regime faced armed rebellion in the north of the country, organised by FROLINAT (Front de Libération Nationale du Tchad). The Gaddafi regime began by backing FROLINAT against Tombalbaye. Then, in 1973, the Libyans occupied the mineral-rich Azou strip in northern Chad. In March 1974, Gaddafi visited Tombalbaye and the two countries issued a declaration of friendship. After Tombalbaye was deposed, the Libyans recognised the new regime of General Felix Malloum but backed FROLINAT against him. By 1978, the guerrillas were having such success that Malloum appealed to Gaddafi to stop the rebels. Peace talks followed, amid allegations that Libya was continuing to fund FROLINAT. FROLINAT, however, faced with the growing possibility of its being able to form a government, split with the Libyans. In March 1979, the Malloum government fell, to be replaced by one dominated by ex-FROLINAT insurgents, and a ceasefire was declared. But in June 1979, a 2,500-strong Libyan force invaded northern Chad, and the Libyans began to fund secessionist groups in the south of the country.

In August 1979, the southern secessionists were incorporated in a new government. But by March 1980, fighting had broken out again between supporters of President Goukouni Oueddei and supporters of Defence Minister Hissein Habré. Libya gave Goukouni strong military support; Habré was (temporarily) defeated; and the Libyans established a 15,000-strong garrison in the country. In November 1981, after Goukouni had rejected a Libyan proposal for merging Chad with Libya, the Libyan troops were withdrawn and an Organisation of African Unity peacekeeping force established.

The fighting continued, however, and in June 1982, Habré

took the capital N'Djamena and Goukouni fled the country. But by June 1983, Goukouni's forces, backed by Libya, were once again in control of much of the north of the country. Habré appealed for international assistance. The US, Egypt, Sudan, Zaire and France responded with cash. Government troops forced the rebels to retreat, but by August, backed by Libyan air power, Goukouni's forces were once again advancing. Habré once again appealed for help, and this time French President François Mitterand sent 3,000 troops, ostensibly to act as military instructors. The fragile ceasefire established after the French intervention lasted until January 1984. In the course of new fighting, a French aircraft was shot down: the French responded by pushing the Libyan-Goukouni forces north.

In May 1984 Gaddafi offered to withdraw from Chad if Mitterand did the same. Mitterand agreed, and in mid-November it was announced that both countries' troops had left, though the US claimed that 3,000 Libyan troops were still there. Forces hostile to the Habré regime remained in control of much of the north of the country and sporadic fighting continues to this day, in spite of the severe famine which hit Chad from late 1984.

Gaddafi's interventions in Chad were motivated by grandiose desires similar to those which guided his attempts to merge Libya with other Arab states. He believed that the Islamic nations of sub-Saharan Africa should unite to form a single giant Islamic republic. He backed the POLISARIO guerrillas against the Moroccans in Western Sahara from the early 1970s (though in June 1983, to dissuade Hassan from sending troops to Chad to support Habré, he dropped his support for POLISARIO and patched up relations with Hassan, signing a friendship treaty in 1984). He has backed Malian oppositionists both financially and militarily. In 1979 he financed and trained Islamic fundamentalist guerrillas operating in Senegal. In 1980 he turned his attentions to Gambia, again training and financing Islamic guerrillas. There is also some evidence that Gaddafi supported Jerry Rawlings' 1981 coup in Ghana – though recently he has criticised the Ghanian regime. With the exception of POLISARIO (which in any case relies rather more on Algerian than on Libyan support), none of these destabilisation attempts have met with success. As each badly planned plot has been uncovered, the government in question has temporarily broken diplomatic ties with Libya and expelled alleged Libyan subversives.

Elsewhere in Africa, Libyan interventions have been similarly inconsequential. Gaddafi gave support to the Amin regime in Uganda, where Libyan troops ended up fighting (unsuccessfully) to prevent the overthrow of Amin in 1979. Libya has also given aid to Eritrean nationalists fighting the Soviet-backed regime (as has the US) and to anti-government groups in Kenya.

The Iran-Iraq War Libya has supported Iran in the Gulf War since 1980 and has been a major supplier of arms. This has exacerbated Libyan isolation in the Arab world.

The empire strikes back

Gaddafi's exploits in the Middle East and North Africa (and to a lesser extent the activities of the People's Bureaux in Europe and the US) increasingly antagonised Western governments during the late 1970s and 1980s. The US in particular saw the Libyan regime as a thorn in its flesh.

In 1979, Gaddafi threatened a cut-off in oil supplies to the US after President Carter, angered by Libyan involvement in Chad, introduced export restrictions on agricultural and electronic equipment and civilian aircraft. In December the same year, the US embassy in Tripoli was sacked by demonstrators protesting against the US playing host to the exiled Shah of Iran. The US responded by withdrawing its ambassador to Libya. In May 1980, Gaddafi threatened another embargo, this time on the US, Britain and Italy, as a means of extracting compensation for war damage suffered by Libya during the Second World War. Relations with the US deteriorated further in 1981. In January, the Libyan People's Bureau in the US was closed. The Reagan administration made it clear that it objected to the Libyan presence in Chad, and in August US fighter aircraft shot down two Libyan jets which had intercepted them in the Gulf of Sidra. In December 1981, Reagan claimed that he had the names of a Libyan 'hit squad' which had been sent to assassinate him, and in March 1982 the administration announced that the US Sixth Fleet would exercise in the Gulf of Sidra, despite Gaddafi's statements that any such action would be considered an act of war.

Faced with this US offensive, Gaddafi turned to the Eastern

bloc for support. Already a big customer for Soviet arms, Libya concluded friendship agreements with the USSR, Czechoslovakia, Poland, Bulgaria and Romania in 1982-83. Gaddafi also made attempts to improve relations with pro-Western Arab regimes, visiting Saudi Arabia, North Yemen, Jordan and Morocco in June 1983.

Relations with the West continued to sour. In 1984, the People's Bureau in London was expelled after shots fired at anti-Gaddafi demonstrators from one of its windows killed a British policewoman. The war of words with Reagan reached new peaks of rhetorical excess, with Gaddafi calling on American blacks to overthrow Reagan by force of arms and Reagan accusing Gaddafi of being the source of world terrorism. In 1986, the Reagan administration once again sent the Sixth Fleet into the Gulf of Sidra. The rest of the story is well known.

What effect the American raid will have on the Gaddafi regime is difficult to tell. It has not succeeded in weakening Gaddafi's position, let alone wiping Gaddafi from the face of the earth. Indeed, it seems as if the domestic position of his regime and its popularity in the Arab world have been strengthened by the attack. The raid has pushed Gaddafi into seeking closer alignment with the Soviet bloc. Unsurprisingly, however, the Soviet Union has responded rather coolly to his advances. Gaddafi remains as internationally isolated as ever.

He continues to be vulnerable to coups, US airstakes and 'covert operations' and (in the long term at least) rising popular discontent. But, after the raid, there is neither more nor less reason than before to expect that his regime, a unique hybrid product of authoritarian populist mobilisation, anti-colonist Arab nationalism, Islamic traditionalism, haphazard state planning and oil wealth, will not be with us for some time yet.

THE VIEW FROM THE MIDDLE EAST

Sanaa Osseiran

The American attack on Libya took place during the fourth month of the UN Year of Peace, a year supposed to be dedicated to the promotion of peace all over the world. The American attack was not only a violation of the spirit of the UN, but also indicated an erosion of the rule of law in the world. Forty years ago, the US was one of the founders of the United Nations and its main financial contributor. Today, the continuous US violation of the UN Charter exposes the limitations of this organisation when faced with a rich and determined superpower and the danger to world peace from such acts as the raids on Libya.

Since President Reagan came to power, the American administration has taken a bellicose attitude on many issues. The aggression against Libya is seen as further proof of their disregard for justice and peace in the world. People in the Middle East consider that the US exercises state terrorism, in the name of fighting terrorism. They also think this of Israel. Both countries talk of the necessity of combating terrorism, but neither has proposed a study of the causes of terrorism in the Middle East. Terrorism goes back to time immemorial; it is not merely a contemporary issue. This is especially true in the Middle East. After the First World War, the Zionists used terrorism in Palestine. These terrorists, as they were designated by the British mandatory power at the time, were considered freedom fighters by their fellow Zionists. Similarly, all liberation movements that came on the international scene used terrorist means to achieve their national aims. The key to the Libyan affair, from an Arab point of view, is whether the Palestinians and Lebanese can achieve their goals other than by terrorism. Most of those involved in committing such acts in the past two years, who have been used by Gaddafi, are young men who have lost everything as a result of

Israeli bombardment and American complicity and who have found all other outlets blocked.

This chapter will reflect on some of the reactions of Arab public opinion to the American aggression, its likely consequences and the possibilities for remedying the current state of affairs, and will propose certain goals for the European peace movements in the immediate future.

The American aggression was condemned by all Arab governments. While it may be true that certain Arab governments were not altogether displeased that Colonel Gaddafi was being taught a lesson, they had to take into account the reactions of their people, which is what I will concentrate on. Mass demonstrations were not allowed in most Arab countries, although spontaneous protest took place despite this. In Tunisia, demonstrators clashed with the police as they shouted anti-American slogans and political leaders who are not known for their pro-Libyan sympathies protested vigorously against the raids. The Tunisians have a specific reason for anti-American feeling. They have not yet swallowed the humiliation of the Israeli raid on the PLO headquarters in Tunis in October 1985, where 74 people died. Twelve of them were Tunisians. No Arab national, conscious of the humiliation inflicted, can forget how the White House described the Israeli attack, as a 'legitimate response' and an expression of self-defence against terrorist attacks. President Reagan said 'I have always had great confidence in the Israeli secret service information'. Naturally, these statements were revised later on, as President Reagan's advisers measured the result they would have on one of the staunchest allies in the Maghreb, President Bourguiba.

Spontaneous demonstrations also took place in Khartoum, the Sudanese capital. Around two thousand demonstrators protested against US aggression and one American diplomat was shot and wounded. This could have been worse had it not been for police reinforcements around the US Embassy. The slogans shouted were not for Gaddafi, but for the struggle of the Libyan people. The Sudanese people, like the Libyans, feel humiliated by the Americans. The US supported dictator Numeiry for 16 years, and the great financial scandal that surrounded the exodus of the Falasha Jews from Ethiopia through Sudan in 1985 added to this anti-American feeling. It is now well known that the US government facilitated their exodus to Israel and that many US organizations bribed Numeiry and his entourage for this purpose.

Examples in various countries illustrate the Arab people's attitude towards the US. Gaddafi will be supported in his defiance and excused for his acts because of what is happening in the Arab world at the joint hands of Israel and the US. One was the *Achille Lauro* affair in October 1985, where the US intercepted an Egyptian airliner. The demonstrations in Cairo reflected the anger and humiliation felt by the Egyptian people. The President, Hosni Mubarak, had to take action to calm the crowds. The Egyptian military policeman in Sinai who recently shot six Israeli tourists was called by the Egyptian government the 'mad' policeman. But his act could be interpreted as one of individual retaliation. He was considered as a 'martyr' by the Egyptian masses after his suicide and the strange circumstances that surrounded his death.

The Israeli destruction of the Iraqi nuclear reactor is another example which illustrates how the US and Israel apply their own laws to the world to suit their ambitions. The Israelis justified their action on the grounds of security, self-defence, liberty and democracy. An Arab commentator in the Lebanese newspaper *Al-Safir* described the AWAC reconnaissance aircraft stationed in Saudi Arabia as the AWACS with one eye. The Americans claim the AWACS did not see or know about the Israeli attack on the Iraqi reactor although Israeli planes crossed into Saudi airspace. But the same AWACS witnessed the Iranian attack on the Kuwaiti oil fields.

Worst of all was the Israeli invasion of Lebanon, when 20,000 Lebanese and Palestinians were killed during the 28-day siege of Beirut, and when Israel annexed a strip of southern Lebanon. The families of those killed cannot and will not forget what Israel did to their children, mothers and brothers with their bombs – made in the US. The report of the MacBride Commission on the Israeli invasion of Lebanon (August-November 1982) describes the types of bombs used by Israeli aircraft. You need to read the reports to comprehend the extent of anti-Israeli and anti-American feelings evoked, to understand the need to resist powers which dictate their terms and refuse to face the roots of the problems for all people in the region.

I have given these examples to explain why the Arab press branded the American attack on Libya as a further example of Israeli-American contempt for the Arabs. A furious parallel was drawn with the tripartite aggression against Egypt in 1956, during the Suez war. The Arab press argues that the US, by its action, has raised Gaddafi's standing in the Arab and Islamic world, instead of weakening it.

Suleiman Ferali wrote in a leading article in *Al-Sayyad*, which is not a left-wing magazine,

> that the American view of the world is an arrogant one and it is addressed against the Arabs and the Muslims. It is a racist attitude and perhaps this is the real secret of the complementarity of view between the American and Israeli policies.

He went on to indicate how the world must be

> shivering with fear from this diabolical situation which in the name of fighting terrorism is committing real terrorism. The world is forced to choose a situation of war so that the US can impose conditions that serve its own interests. The US does not even take into consideration her traditional allies in the area; only Israel's opinion weighs in the American vision of the world today.

This magazine also says that the US has given itself the divine right to teach the world as if it were 'God's chosen policeman' (an ironic reference to the 'chosen people'). Yet another leading article considered that the American aggression in Libya has given the people of the Middle East a rare opportunity to understand what has happened in Iran and Afghanistan, and the way in which the cultural centre of Lebanon was destroyed to create conditions in which the people of the East can be classified as barbaric and Israel seen as the beacon of democracy.

Another theme was the role of US terrorism when it supports movements such as the 'contras' in Nicaragua and Savimbi's

UNITA in Angola. One has only to recall the role of the US in Chile, in 1973, in overthrowing Salvador Allende and installing military regimes in Latin America. Some papers considered that America is going back to the John Foster Dulles/Stalin era – 'Who is not with us, is against us.'

A more concrete and repeated theme in the Arab press is the new American political and military strategy of forcing Arabs into bilateral negotiations with Israel. Amin-Il-Sibaii wrote in *Al-Hawadeth*, published in London, that the strategy is aimed at reinforcing American military presence in the Gulf, and that the American attacks on the Gulf of Sidra, justified in terms of the right to free navigation, are a prelude to further American military actions in the Straits of Hermous, on the same grounds. This strategy is seen not only as provocative to the Arab world, but, in the context of superpower rivalry, as bringing the danger of a confrontation between them in this region. The Arab press also touched on the difference of attitude to Libya between some Europeans and the Americans. They attributed French government policy to concern about the fate of the French hostages in Lebanon.

Other articles stressed American hypocrisy in dealing with Libya. For example, in spite of economic sanctions, US branch companies operating in Libya continued their operations. The US is influenced first by its commercial interests and needs of the attitudes of multinational corporations. Several US companies were exempted from the sanctions decision, as were US citizens working for oil companies from the evacuation order. Around 1,000 US citizens have remained in Libya. One of the major reasons why the Europeans refused to go along with US sanctions was precisely the argument that the US has continuously maintained economic relations with Libya and was even its privileged economic partner until recently, despite its accusations that Gaddafi supported terrorism. We could argue that as long as oil was needed on the US market, America maintained a positive attitude towards Gaddafi and his erratic behaviour and Islamic fervour did not seem to create much of a problem. The idea perhaps was that a fervent Muslim leader is a good check against communism. This is possibly the only good thing about Islam for the Americans and Israelis, who think an Islam of Numeiry's style is good, for it keeps these backward societies dormant. Unfortunately, the more the US and Israel follow this strategy, the more Islamic fundamentalism is likely to grow. Indeed one wonders whether such fundamentalism is not part of their strategy in order to provide moral excuses for their intervention. In the Arab world, this phenomenon is directly linked with the backlash against the US-Israeli strategic alliance. It is no surprise that Iranian fundamentalism has spread in the area and encouraged other Muslim fundamentalists, particularly in Egypt, Southern Lebanon, Tunisia, Morocco and Sudan. It is no surprise that the Iranians sent a message to the Kuwaiti government proposing the necessity of helping an Islamic state (Libya) against American aggression. It is not surprising that the religion is penetrating the Palestinian movement as an alternative form of Arab unity against Israel and the United States.

One has to understand that resort to religion as a means of self-defence is not a new phenomenon. It was used to rally European Jews to Zionism and the return to Zion. Likewise, the Muslims use the concept of Jihad or holy war against the infidels. In the past, 'infidels' was used to describe the European Crusaders. Today, Jihad is used in the context of national aspirations rather than in a strictly religious sense. Libyan radio has called for an Arab and Muslim Jihad against US and Zionist aggression. Similarly the State Department, three hours before the raid took place, dictated an editorial to the Voice of America to be transmitted on its Arabic service 15 times, starting 15 minutes after the raid commenced. It called in implicit terms for the overthrow of the Libyan regime. The point is that the US uses the same methods as Gaddafi. But there is one difference: the US is a superpower which should have a moral responsibility to sustain peace in the world and to find alternative ways to isolate someone like Gaddafi, and not act according to the logic of nineteenth-century empires. Even so, past European empires were far more subtle and intelligent in directing the affairs of the world than the US has been since the 1960s.

When one contemplates the plethora of American technology used against Libya, one cannot help but laugh at the way the US has made itself ridiculous. Libya is a small country of little over three million inhabitants. Perhaps the United States intended to test Soviet reaction, or to prove that the Soviet Union will not risk war for the sake of its allies. But, if this argument is true, isn't the US provoking the Soviet Union, thus threatening peace and stability in the world? Can the Americans guarantee that the Soviet Union will not intervene if Syria is attacked, or for that matter Iran, which has such a long border with the USSR? Or has the US taken the law of the whole world into its hands, regardless of what this might mean for mankind? The Syrian government has reacted strongly against President Reagan's remarks linking Syria and Iran with terrorism and threatening the possibility of retaliation. The Arab press also expressed the fear that the aggression in Libya is the first in a series of actions intended to destabilize still further the Middle East region so as to implement Israeli or American policies against any possible Soviet advancement.

The immediate and future perspectives are very dim. Terrorist actions will certainly increase and nothing will stop them as long as this bellicose attitude is maintained, and as long as the real causes of terrorism are not solved.

A possible role for the European peace movement

It is not far fetched to claim that a nuclear war can erupt in the Middle East or because of the Middle East, considering that Israel has a nuclear capacity and that it intended to use it in the past (1973) had it not been for US military aid. Mr Simha Flappen, head of the Middle Eastern Peace Centre in Tel Aviv, has called for a nuclear-free zone in the Middle East, because of the danger of a nuclear confrontation between the superpowers. There is a growing realization that the threat to world peace does not necessarily emanate from the West, but that disarmament in Europe, while essential, is secondary to the dangers from local and regional conflicts. Ironically, Israel, right after its bombardment of the nuclear reactor in Iraq, called on the Arab states to demilitarise the Middle East region. The Israelis reserve for themselves the nuclear option to strike, but refuse to sign the Non-Proliferation Treaty, thus forcing the Arabs to buy more and more arms, most of the time obsolete arms, instead of really attempting to solve the issues that have caused terrorism. We are witnessing today the emergence of a new form of political anti-semitism which is closing all doors to a peaceful option. This is due to the refusal to see the roots of the problems in the Arab and Islamic world. The fate of those Jews and Western citizens in the Arab world is a reaction to the lack of sensitivity towards the Arab people.

The European peace movement could play an important role in clarifying the issues in the Western world, particularly among American and Israeli public opinion. Firstly it should attempt to strengthen and co-ordinate its ties with the American peace movement, so that information is disseminated about the Palestinian-Israeli conflict, about Lebanon and other vital issues used to camouflage or to hide US and Israeli political and military strategies. Secondly, the European peace movement should encourage the peace movement in Israel by backing its members in their attempt to influence and enlighten Israeli public opinion to recognise the legitimate rights of the Palestinian people to their state. General Harkabi, who used to be the head of Israeli military intelligence, and is now Professor of International Relations at Jerusalem University, is calling for recognition of the Palestinians. He has written, 'To demand a solution for the conflict without the PLO is equal to a state of no solution at all.' The European peace movement should support people of his kind, and work as an intermediary between them and the Palestinian people as a prelude to the creation of a climate that might culminate in a true process for peace. The European peace movement should aim to obtain from the Israeli government a definition of its borders and its security so that people in Lebanon, particularly southern Lebanese, will be reassured that Israeli leaders have no expansionist designs to occupy South Lebanon up to the city of Saida. Furthermore the peace movement should not shy away from the possibility of contacts with the so-called Muslim fundamentalists, even if the idea might be abhorrent to them. They should attempt a dialogue with these people. For Islam is and will remain an important rallying factor for years to come, and among these people are the intelligent, the wise and the terrorist. If there is dialogue, then there is a bridge between people of different modes of thinking and perhaps it will lead to more understanding of the futility of terrorism on one side and the sensitivity of the issues and the future of the people of the region on the other side. The European movement needs to be sensitive, for example, to the fact that there are more than 2,000 people who have disappeared in Lebanon, whose fate is still not known. Some are in Israeli prisons, others may be with different Lebanese militias. Thus, the question of foreign hostages should be treated on an equal level with the suffering of Lebanese and Palestinian families. It is possible that the peace movement could co-ordinate its activities with the International Information Centre on Humanitarian Rights during War, which was created in Paris in September 1982 after the Israeli invasion of the Lebanon.

Another form of action open to the European peace movement is to invite ordinary people of all nations in the Middle East and let them speak about the loss of their children, what war has meant to each and why they support certain movements, and try to distil something from such encounters on a common platform. Perhaps an issue, an idea, can emerge. The peace movement should contact Arabs from different countries so that they may understand the diversity that exists in the Arab world, the specificity of each country and the common problems that bind them together. In this manner, it would initiate a path of trust and confidence between people of different ethnic and religious groups.

Finally, Western democratic societies are based on the assumption that people share in their government's decisions, particularly those decisions that entail the citizen's sacrifice of his or her life in the name of defending and safeguarding democratic ideals. Thus, one should expect from the European peace movement a more vigorous demand for a role in the vital decisions of their states. This will guarantee that those who take decisions are not a handful who decide on war, but parliamentary institutions and people who are the core of a real democracy.

THE WESTERN PEACE MOVEMENT AND THE MIDDLE EAST

Fiona Weir

I was living in Egypt when Israel invaded Lebanon in 1982. Every night for months, my television screen was filled with images of atrocity: the systematic destruction of a densely populated capital city, followed by the Sabra and Shatilla massacres. Although I saw nothing advising Egyptians of their duty to their fellow Arabs, and although no one seemed quite sure how anyone knew where to go, every day I saw queues formed outside the Lebanese Students' Union as Egyptians gathered to give blood for Lebanese hospitals. Some donors had to be persuaded not to go back again the next day. Frustrations ran high at the feebleness of the Egyptian government response.

Friends in Britain, aware of my peacenik leanings, kept me well supplied with clippings and articles from the British peace movement press. But I failed to find a single reference to any protest from the peace movement, any vigil outside the Israeli Embassy, any statements by leading peace movement representatives.

Yet after the raids on Libya, CND's switchboards were jammed as angry members phoned in to find out what they could do, where they could demonstrate: in one day CND received £25,000 in donations.

The West European peace movement of the 1980s began as a response to the 1979 NATO decision to deploy cruise and Pershing missiles in five European countries. At first, the movement was understandably obsessed with nukes to the exclusion of all else. Nuclear weapons, even if they are the ugly symptoms of profound political realities, evoke a powerful gut reaction. The possibility of nuclear war in itself frightens, angers, sickens. Thousands of people of all political beliefs (and many who, at least at first, considered themselves apolitical) demonstrated, blocked roads and wrote to members of Parliament in a massive attempt to change the policies of unresponsive governments. But politics are ever-changing. Since the early 1980s, new issues have forced themselves on to the political agenda, many of them of obvious relevance to the peace movements but with no neat nuclear connection.

Single-issue campaigns tend to respond badly to new issues. They tend to skirt round them, avoiding serious political discussion for fear of damaging the single-issue consensus and dividing the movement. Reactions tend to be slow and awkward, and analysis weak. Thus, CND's first resolution on the Middle East, passed in 1985, concentrated exclusively on Israeli nuclear weapons, Israel's links with South Africa, and the bombing of the Iraqi nuclear power station in 1981. It missed the point. Opposition to the Israeli nuclear programme is certainly necessary, particularly in the light of the absence of internal opposition and Israel's refusal to sign the Non-Proliferation Treaty or accept the control of the International Atomic Energy Authority. But until the Israelis nuclearise battlefield weapons or the Arabs develop a nuclear capability, the threat to peace in the Middle East is not primarily nuclear and is anyway essentially a result of the superpowers' political and military strategies and the failure to resolve the political conflicts of the region.

Of course, there is a real danger of superpower nuclear confrontation developing from war in the Third World.Of 19 documented instances of threatened use of nuclear weapons, 13 were in the Third World, five of them in the Middle East. During the 1973 Arab-Israeli war, the world-wide alert of US strategic forces brought us up to DEFCON-3, two steps away from thermonuclear war. What's more, since the Vietnam war, Americans have displayed a certain reluctance to see their boys killed. This worthy sentiment, all too rarely extended to non-Americans, has created the problem of how to deploy adequate military strength to maintain a 'progressive and integrated world economy' in the face of revolutions, border wars, and misguided leaders unable to perceive the benefits of the US embrace. And so . . . But perhaps we should let US strategists damn themselves. Vice-Admiral Gerald E. Miller, in Congressional testimony in March 1976, stated:

> It will become increasingly difficult in the near future to protect US overseas interests with conventional weapons. It may well be that the threat of the use of, at least, tactical nuclear weapons is the only option available to us . . . I have in mind situations that are far from our shores, where we would have difficulty, from a logistics point of view, at least, in reaching the areas in which we would have a considerable US interest . . . In no way do I subscribe to the basic assumption that even a so-called modest use of tactical nuclear weapons would inevitably lead to a full all-out nuclear war. There are many situations where one or more weapons could be used without escalation. I have in mind, particularly, situations where the exchange might take place at sea or where warning shots are fired in the atmosphere or desolated areas.

But exclusive concern about the 'deadly connection' between intervention in the Third World and the likelihood of a nuclear conflict starting in one of the world's flashpoints is not enough: to be blunt, it is merely staring obsessively at the symptoms. As an American peace movement delegation to the Middle East put it:

> Witness to the anguished debate among all sides involved in this regional conflict, we return with a deepened understanding of the myriad ways in which the superpowers contending throughout the world, broker power and influence, accelerate the arms race, exacerbate local hostilities, and inhibit peaceful resolution of local conflicts. An analysis of the deadly connection thus extends beyond the recognition that a nuclear war might be triggered in an area of regional unrest. The dynamics of the Cold War – the Soviet Union pitted against the US, vying for influence, creating dependencies and polarizing local factions – exacerbate the tensions. It is critical that those of us who wish to reduce the risk of nuclear war, oppose the foreign policies that are maintained by nuclear weapons and make their use more likely.

A nuclear war, in other words, would result from a particular political situation: the greatest danger to world peace at present is not the nukes themselves, but rather the political confrontation of the two superpowers, exacerbated by the current mood in the United States, and the superpowers' unwillingness to seek out the causes of conflict, their preference for throwing military might at problems.

Of course, the peace movement has begun to understand all this. For five years the mainstream tendency of the European peace movements has called for the breakdown of the bloc system that divides Europe in two. But, on the whole, the peace movements haven't related their understanding of the Cold War in Europe to the rest of the world. Yet, just as Europe has suffered from alignment into two armed and hostile blocs, so the Middle East has felt the effects of deep-rooted political and military confrontations – not just between the two superpowers but between Israel and the Arabs over the Palestinian question.

To many in the Middle East, peace is a discredited word. Most of the Arab world associates it with the 1977 Camp David agreement between Israel and Egypt, which is seen as a means of promoting US interests in the region and neutralising Egypt. Few analysts of the Middle East see any hope for a lasting peace until the fundamental causes of instability are eradicated. Quite simply, there is a people too many or a state too few. Without denying the importance of other conflicts – both between and within states – the Palestinian question and the related militarism of Israel are seen as the heart of the problem.

The Palestinian question is riven with suspicions and memories of past atrocities. Military solutions have become less and less viable. Forced expulsions, intimidation, and attempts to deny the existence of the Palestinian people have all failed. They will not go away. Nor are Arab regimes in any position to inflict severe military defeat on the Israelis and the PLO has no bases for attacks. Two peoples are demanding the right to self-determination in a state in the same area.

Proposals for settlement of the Palestinian question abound. To a large extent the success of any of these will depend on internal forces in Israeli society. Growing Zionist extremism and the long-term effects of being an occupying power are cause for pessimism about the influence of beleagured Israeli peace opinion. How long Palestinians, particularly in the West Bank and Gaza, can continue and develop effective resistance to occupation and expulsions, and the extent to which the PLO can maintain unity and draw creative lessons from the past are also open to question. The PLO (an umbrella group of organisations) is the only recorded political movement in history to be recognised by more governments than its governmental adversary, but has been strikingly unsuccessful in thwarting Israeli expansion. Its durability and overwhelming support, especially inside the occupied territories, is a measure of the legitimacy it has among Palestinians. No settlement will be acceptable to the Palestinian people which is not agreed by direct negotiations with the PLO – they recognise no other group as having any right to represent them.

Palestinian political scientist Bichara Khader has written that

> the result of being constantly pulled in opposite directions has been to create permanent tensions within the Arab world. In these circumstances Europe appears as a lifeline for an Arab world drowning in East-West enmity and pounded by the machinations of the great powers.

Europe cannot escape involvement in the Middle East. Historically, economically and politically, European countries have strong ties with the region. But, Khader argues 'Europe has blown hot and cold over the Middle East conflict, making complete reversals in policy, procrastinating and perpetuating the ambiguities in its position.' He identifies American perceptions of even the slightest degree of European autonomy as a threat to their leadership, as being the main barrier to the formation of an independent stance.

The story of the most recent European initiative, the EEC Venice Declaration of 1980 is a case in point. It called for Israeli withdrawal from all territories occupied in 1967, and declared settlements in these territories illegal under international law and a serious obstacle to peace. The Palestinians were recognised as having legitimate national rights, and a comprehensive peace settlement to permit self-determination was considered necessary. The PLO was to be associated with the negotiations.

Israel and the US were both determined to block the Venice

Declaration and by mid-1982 it had been effectively shelved. A belated but 'vigorous condemnation' of the Israeli invasion of Lebanon was spelt out at a European Council meeting in Brussels in June 1982, reaffirming the main principles of the Venice Declaration, but in a much weaker form. Thatcher's response to the visit of Mohamed Milhem and Bishop Khouri (both known to be linked with the PLO leadership) in October 1985 underlined continuing confusion as to what a European role in the peace process should be. Just before a meeting with the British government was due to happen, Thatcher imposed conditions not mentioned in the Foreign Office invitation to the two men, in an attempt to satisfy both US and European opinion. She failed to satisfy anyone.

Yet there is the potential for Europe to play a major role in bringing peace to the Middle East. The question for the peace movements is how they can act to persuade their governments to play such a role.

There are several key demands with regard to the Middle East, which would find a fair amount of consensus with the peace movement: denuclearisation of the Mediterranean – both the Israeli and superpower nukes; assertion of the Palestinian right to self-determination through an independent Palestinian state; recognition of the right of all states in the area to exist with security guarantees; the demand for an international peace conference bringing together all concerned parties, including the PLO and the Soviet Union. European governments need to be pushed on all of these. Though desirable, demilitarisation of the area, beyond superpower build-down, is unlikely until the cause of tensions and the Palestinian problem are addressed. In addition the peace movement can build upon its considerable experience of dialogue with East Europeans to break down the bipolar bloc mentality and stereotyped images. There is a natural desire to ask who our counterparts are in different regions of the world, in the absence of a 'peace movement' which conforms to our own assumptions. Practical priorities differ, as do the causes for which people are willing to take risks. Having understood the preoccupations of independent East European peace activists with civil liberties, we are less likely to postulate conditions, more able to draw the links.

Some tentative steps have been made. A peace movement conference on the Middle East in the Netherlands this year revealed how intractable some of the problems were. Most delegates were convinced that their organisations should recognise the PLO; most were hesitant to put it on their agenda. At the END Convention in 1985, Dutch peace movement leader Mient Jan Faber, commenting on the presence of representatives from liberation movements, said

> We all sympathised with their struggles, but the precise ins and outs of the various problems, not to mention the solutions which must be sought, were mostly foreign to us. That gave them a rather romantic tint, as if they had just walked out of an exciting book.

The loudest burst of applause during Meg Beresford's speech at a 1985 conference on the peace movements and the Third World came when she asked, 'Why can we register our liberal concerns over Ethiopia and keep quiet about what is going on in Handsworth, and about the war that is going on in Northern Ireland?' – though she added that 'this is not because I want CND to start campaigning on Northern Ireland, but to point out that we are selective in our concerns.' On the principle that the hip bone's attached to the thigh bone, there is an enormous shopping list of injustices the peace movement could heave on to its well-laden back and some good rows to be had as light is cast on the greyer areas. Racism and the position of immigrant workers are now firmly on the agenda of several European groups, as are civil liberties. A grassroots movement has to find ways of assimilating the 'specialist elites' it throws up as the need for expertise grows. Policy has to be geared to people's ability to make links with their own concerns, campaign in localities and overcome the disempowering effect of complex issues.

Reaction to the raid on Libya was easier for the peace movement than working out a coherent political response to the Middle East and all its problems. People were angry and morally outraged. Of course, moral outrage is fundamental to the peace movement, and it does little harm to express it. Our colour supplements burst with yet more blood each week. The protests throughout the week after the bombing, the sit-down in Grosvenor Square and blockade of Oxford Street, showed a well of anti-militarist sentiment deeper than any immediate nuclear connections.

But Noam Chomsky's warning, written in September 1982 after the Israeli invasion of the Lebanon, remains as apposite as ever: if the disarmament movement of the Western world continues to duck the question of Palestine and the issues arising out of Israel's transformation into a major military power allied to the United States, it 'dooms itself to near irrelevance'.

RETHINKING COUNTER-TERRORISM

Richard Falk

Terrorism is many-faceted, and has a heritage that can be traced back to the poisoning of wells and assassination plots of ancient times. Many uses of political violence are described as 'terrorism' by their adversaries or intended victims. I have even heard a prominent international business executive describe as terrorism expropriations of foreign property in Chile during the Allende years. My preoccupation in this essay is with international terrorism, that is, with incidents which have a transnational character by involving nationals or territory of more than one country. This excludes Basque or Sikh struggles for autonomy, or secession struggles carried on in the main within the borders of a single country, and involving a form of conflict between state and civil society. To limit the focus to the special character of the US/Libyan conflict, I also emphasize only those forms of international terrorism which possess a First World/Third World structure, and include a prominent element of governmental or state sponsorship. Thus, despite their international ties and locus of operations, this essay does not deal with the issues posed by such urban terrorist groups as the Red Brigades, Japanese Red Army Faction, or Baader-Meinhof gang. These exclusions are admittedly somewhat arbitrary and artificial, as part of the inflamed Euro-American climate on the topic of terrorism was established by the period of intense activity on the part of these groups. Also, these groups often claimed inspiration from liberation struggles in the Third World.

Statist orientations towards political violence label as 'terrorism' those acts done by unauthorised or underground groups on a covert basis and designed to spread fear among the general population. An official publication of the US State Department, *Patterns of Global Terrorism*, proposes such a definition:

> Terrorism is premeditated, politically motivated violence perpetrated against noncombatant targets by subnational groups or clandestine state agents, usually intended to influence an audience.

As might be expected, these images of terrorism play down the role of overt state violence, regardless of its indiscriminateness or its intent to hit 'noncombatant targets'. These forms of state sponsorship are generally treated as falling within the morally neutral and emotively positive category of 'uses of force' or 'military action'. At least the State Department definition encompasses clandestine statist connections and covert operations, and so would include the role of the CIA and other intelligence agencies in planning, guiding and carrying out violent schemes against noncombatants.

There is also some inconsistency in the classification of behaviour. This US definition would presumably exclude violence directed at military personnel, but the report to which it is attached specifically counts as 'terrorism' violence of the sort described even if the targets are 'combatant' (that is, military personnel police, or official representatives of the foreign societies). A more restrictive view would distinguish between belligerent violence against military targets in an armed struggle and violence deliberately directed at civilians and designed to shock and scare the general populace.

In the Libyan case, the sponsoring connection was alleged to have many aspects: ideological encouragement, training and equipping, logistic support overseas in diplomatic facilities, transmission of weapons, safe havens for accused terrorists, overseas assassinations of political opponents, and even specific directives. In the foreground, of course, was the flamboyant person of Colonel Muammar al Gaddafi, who seemed to embrace anti-US terrorism as the central tenet of his foreign policy, and called on terrorists to strike at US and Israeli targets. Even sceptics must grant Washington a strong *prima facie* basis for its charges that Libya and its leaders are definitely sponsors of state terrorism, and that the Soviet Union lurks approvingly somewhere in the background.

Yet even here the situation is more complicated than it might seem. Over the years, the United States has a poor track record with all Third World nationalist leaders who claim the full plenum of sovereign rights for their country and try to build some kind of wider regional community by invoking a radical nationalist ideology. Whether one looks back to Nasser, Nkrumah, or Sukarno the story is more or less the same, and even a pro-Western statesman like Nehru was derided by Washington as 'immoral' merely because he advocated a diplomacy of non-alignment for the non-Western world of Asia and Africa. Mossadegh Arbenz and Allende fared even worse, provoking covert US-sponsored interventions that drove them from power and put in their place cruel and brutal regimes. The United States has never been able to accept the legitimacy of a Third World leader who pursued a genuine nationalist line inhospitable to both international capitalist interests and to the Cold War. Even poor little New Zealand is being given a taste of this bitter herb of American hostility because it dared to distance itself from the nuclear aspects of its alliance with the United States.

Long before Ronald Reagan ever arrived in the White House, Colonel Gaddafi earned the ire of United States' leaders for a host of reasons other than state-sponsored terrorism: closing the large US military base in Libya, moving in on the oil companies, implementing a version of Islamic socialism, boisterously embracing and financing as a social obligation the Palestinian cause in its most radical form, tirelessly promoting anti-Western attitudes in the Third World, intervening throughout his region to displace Western influence and topple 'moderate', that is Western-oriented, leaders. On this basis, the more assertive foreign policy of the Reagan period has put Gaddafi's Libya at the top of its 'enemies list'. It has been a thinly disguised objective of US foreign policy to destabilize and, if possible, to overthrow Gaddafi ever since his administration took office. There have been several sets of menacing naval manoeuvres designed to challenge Libyan claims to the Gulf of Sidra, each of which has enticed Libya into a military exchange that displayed US prowess and superiority in confrontation. In addition, Reagan has frequently engaged in provocative name-calling in his speeches, Libya being classed as an 'outlaw' nation and its leader a 'flake' and a 'barbarian'. Obviously, the intention was to fasten a pariah status on Libya, encouraging to anti-Gaddafi elements in the Libyan army.

In the weeks prior to the 15 April raid, these policies of provocation peaked. In late March, a huge US naval formation began to carry on prolonged manoeuvres. This show of force challenged Gaddafi to respond on behalf of Libya's Gulf of Sidra claim, resulting in some 56 Libyan fatalities and the destruction of Libyan patrol boats and some shore facilities. Less publicised, was Gaddafi's definite effort, after these military engagements, to open diplomatic discussions with Washington. This initiative was brushed aside as worthless ('we have nothing to talk to Tripoli about . . . ') without even a formal response. At the very least, the United States government baited the hook, unquestionably seeking a pretext for military action directed at the vital human centre of Libyan political leadership, delivered in a secret, one-sided, terroristic manner, calculated to stir up whatever embers of opposition existed in Libya. The action also provided a battlefield test for some untried weapons systems, especially the F-111s, and an interventionary tactic of surprise air strikes at night after covering a huge distance. Although the evidence has not yet been confirmed, the Pentagon's enthusiasm for this undertaking is likely to be explained by these features. Recall that Casper Weinberger has been consistently sceptical of uses of military force which could not be validated by 'victory' or by some clear military purpose. In this, Weinberger's view has frequently clashed with, and until the Tripoli/Benghazi raids, prevailed over, the Shultz view that interventionary violence against Third World terrorism was long overdue regardless of specific effects.

At the core of Reagan's counter-terrorism policy is an almost existential primal dread. Justifying the raid on Tripoli, President Reagan reached a climax in his broadcast talk on the night of the attack: 'And for us to ignore, by inaction, the slaughter of American civilians and American soldiers, whether in nightclubs or airline terminals, is simply not in the American tradition.' The following day, in the course of brief remarks at the start of the American Business Conference, Reagan returned to this theme, '. . . we demonstrated once again that doing nothing is not America's policy, it's not the American way.'

Reagan is undoubtedly haunted by a remembrance of Jimmy Carter's fate during the Iranian hostage crisis of 1979-80. He was, as well, being dogged by conservative critics complaining that the rhetoric of the Reagan administration on terrorism was a mask behind which could be found the wimpy visage of Carter. Given his own hype about Gaddafi and the menace he posed for American values and interests, there was indeed public pressure in the United States for retaliatory action once the facts were brought forward to establish a Libyan connection with the bomb explosion of 5 April in the Berlin discotheque. (In passing, it may do to hold back somewhat on accepting 'the facts' on the Berlin incident, especially since the arrest of Jordanian suspects with primarily Syrian ties and the failure to document the alleged telex intercepts that provided Washington with its smoking gun; if it seems childishly conspiratorial to doubt the veracity of Washington on such matters it's as well to remind ourselves that massive falsification of evidence was used by the Reagan people to build up their case against the Soviet Union after the KAL 007 shoot-down incident in 1982, even at the cost of driving the world towards the brink. It is also worth pondering that our whole interpretation of the Libyan attack must be altered if the grounds of Gaddafi's sponsorship of terrorism were themselves trumped up.)

For Americans, as well as for their leadership, doing something about terrorism has become virtually synonymous with taking military action that causes numerous casualties and flaunts a capacity to penetrate sovereign space of Third World countries at will. There were no illusions about effectiveness. No claims were or could be made that this punitive use of military force would stop terrorism. The American public, which gave its approval to the US military action by a margin of 71% to 21%, according to a *Newsweek* poll, lent its support despite believing that the raid would increase terrorist activity in the long run. Thirty-seven per cent of Americans polled actually believed the raid would increase terrorist activity, 24% thought it would have no effect; only 31% believed it would decrease terrorism. These post-attack reactions confirm once again that Reagan construes the political unconscious of the American people better than any president since Franklin Roosevelt. He both reflects its confusions and acts on them with a superb sense of timing. Unhappily, violence unleashed against perceived enemies remains an American character trait.

One disturbing element here is that the United States, confronted by frustration and challenge, not knowing what to do, had mindless recourse to military force despite the contrary counsel of most of its closest allies. Perhaps worse, this insistence on going it alone militarily could not be explained as a resolve to deal a blow against terrorism in a setting where others were scared to act. There is little evidence to suggest that any of the Reagan inner circle believed that such an air strike would abate terrorist activity. On the contrary, as with the public, most expected a rise in terrorist incidents to ensue, and this has indeed happened. In this regard, the mainstream American effort to present the European refusal as 'appeasement' is poor thinking at best and, more likely, knowing and sinister mischief. Let's recall who the Europeans appeased and what the consequences of Munich were for Americans. European squeamishness about military force in the 1930s gave the green light to Hitler and brought on World War II. The United States was isolationist then, but to stand aside now would be to invite the terrorists of the world to become ever bolder until a war ensues, and the Europeans succumb, at least until the United States comes to the rescue at considerable cost to itself. In this regard, with the shining exception of 10 Downing Street, European qualms about military force are a new expression of the spirit of Munich. In a BBC interview on her support for the raid Mrs Thatcher went all-out for the Munich analogy: 'It would have been jolly easy to run away, jolly easy to demonstrate the weakness that we demonstrated in the 1930s.' But she put her case on the ground of solidarity ('friendship is two way . . . '), not on her belief that the US policy would reduce terrorism. The logic of invoking Munich is flawed: the whole point of the critique of appeasement is that if Hitler had been challenged early, Germany would have backed down and presumably confined its ugly behaviour to its own borders. No one makes any sort of comparable claim here.

There is also a subliminal message. Terrorists and their sponsors are 'Nazis', that is, a criminal element which can be destroyed at will, not a proper adversary at all. And indirectly, since the whole of the populace in the Middle East seems to endorse terrorist tactics, there is an indictment of the Third World as such, and especially its Arab and Islamic members. In effect, the moral climate for race war on a permanent basis is being subtly established behind the façade of proceeding against a single crazed leader is reinforced by a series of images currently active in the US popular culture, especially films like *Invasion USA*, *Red Dawn* and the *Rambo* series. In each, a complacent America is ill-prepared for the coming of the barbarians – Third World terrorists somehow managed from Moscow by psychopathic intermediaries. Against these fiendish adversaries anything goes. Normal combat doesn't work. Peaceful methods are absurdly irrelevant. The Reagan anti-terrorist crusade is gearing up for just such a war, which is increasingly being seen as 'the real war'. As such, it supersedes East/West scenarios of World War III and provides the public with relief from anxiety about nuclear war, extermination and the terminal condition of the human race.

On the surface the issues are more calmly considered, yet even the most moderate media pundits seem genuinely relieved that at least some Libyan blood has been spilled on behalf of anti-terrorism. Strobe Talbott of *Time*, for instance, construed the incident as characteristic of the Reagan penchant for 'global unilateralism', suggesting that the disposition to take decisive action by itself in the face of almost universal opposition was '. . . the lot of a superpower'. In this sense, even for Talbott, unilateralism on the part of the United States no longer has a bad name. Such an attitude is expressive of deepening American diplomatic isolation. From 1945 through the Korean War and into the 1950s, United States foreign policy generally received an enthusiastic international blessing in the halls of the United Nations; collective security was the thing. In the 1960s, the Third World began to exert itself, the non-aligned movement became a potent force, and Washington dropped its pretence of internationalism. In the 1960s and 1970s, US foreign policy claimed to be acting out its role as alliance leader in a variety of regional settings; retaining credibility was the thing. This meant invoking the figleaf of SEATO to validate aggression in Vietnam, the OAS for Western hemisphere interventions, but it relied on this community setting to validate its controversial uses of force. Even the Cuban missile crisis of 1962 had its OAS dimension that supposedly conferred legitimacy on US claims.

An irony is that earlier in the post-war period alliance tensions arose from American annoyance with European unilateralism. Eisenhower decided to stay out of the French Indochina war because in 1953 Britain, under Eden, wanted no part of a collective venture on behalf of the beleaguered French. More dramatically, the United States sided with Nasser's Egypt, the arch-villain in the Third World, rather than back the unilateralism of the Suez operation in 1956. The United States lectured its allies on the unacceptability of unilateral military force, whatever the pretext, and threw its weight in the United Nations behind a demand for withdrawal by England, France and Israel. Some have called this American response to Suez the last moral act in international politics. In any event, shifting currents have achieved a Euro-American role reversal that has never been so clear as after the Libyan attack.

Or is it? True, the United Nations Security Council did pass a censure resolution stymied only by the veto of Britain and the United States. But Europe has seemed to be following a much stronger anti-Libyan line after the raid than before it, and has suddenly adopted a co-operative approach to international terrorism. Surely in Washington this new spirit of counter-terrorist co-operation in Europe is interpreted as a solid success which by itself vindicates Reagan's military approach. In effect, even if the Europeans opposed the attack as such, they have at least been awakened after the fact to the dangers they face. Perhaps, here too, the collective subconscious is more active than militarists in Washington suppose. It may be that the Libyan raid and intimations of more to come, possibly next time against Iran or Syria, have bought to the surface a different kind of concern on the part of responsible European leaders. They may perceive Reagan's America as a kind of rogue elephant which could easily produce an overall breakdown in international order with frightful political and economic consequences. As such, it is essential to get the United States back into the herd, even if it means bending European views on the best way to ride out the terrorist storm. The alliance framework functions, then, more to restrain its superpower leader than as a co-operative venture against enemies external to the alliance. If such a switch in gears is really taking place, then the Cold War is truly over, no matter how much anti-Soviet rhetoric is pumped out by the Washington propaganda mills, and a kind of dealignment is in place, genuinely, as a by-product of shifting priorities.

More conventionally, the alliance hierarchy provides an explanation for this apparent adjustment. European governments other than Britain held out against military force, but they quickly settled back into their more familiar roles as subordinate members of NATO. However, it is also true that European official behaviour expresses the widely-shared confusion about what to do about terrorism. The brutal and bloody 27 December attacks on the Vienna and Rome airports underscored the uncomfortable truth that pursuing a pro-Palestinian foreign policy or accommodating approach would not put national territory off-limits even for those terrorist groups associated with the Arab-Israeli struggle. Therefore, while it is necessary for Europe to develop a counter-terrorist policy, it is one thing to refrain from terrorist incitement and another to join in thinning down the Libyan diplomatic presence, co-ordinating intelligence operations and agreeing on procedures to share information and suspects. It is possible to interpret both Europe's refusal and its co-operative stance as elements of an evolving counter-terrorist diplomacy, exhibiting balance and maturity.

A neat summary of what the Reaganites are up to helps us to a better understanding of the attack on Libya. George Will, a most influential conservative analyst, celebrated the attack precisely because it was done against the tide of international public opinion. Will argues that only by 'a healthy, even jaunty disregard for "world opinion" ' can US foreign policy be truly Reaganized, which implies three things:

> One is the Reagan Doctrine: support for resistance movements at the margin of the Soviet Empire (Nicaragua, Angola, Afghanistan); the second involves demonstrating willingness to use military force (Grenada, Libya), even – no, especially – without allied consensus. The third involves restoring realism

by displacing the arms control 'process' as the centerpiece of US-Soviet relations.

To find a popular basis in the US for military action has been the quest of all leaders, whatever their party affiliation, ever since the Vietnam defeat. It is hoped that getting the American people to march in step beneath the banner of anti-terrorism will rebuild enthusiasm for an interventionary foreign policy. The Libyan attack, as was the Grenada invasion, is a testing of the American people. Can their satisfaction with a quick and painless military victory be extended to other, more problematic settings? Both the Gulf of Sidra provocation at the end of March and the Tripoli attack were timed to occur suspiciously close to crucial votes in Congress on the issue of extending yet another $100 million in support of the 'contras'. But the Vietnam syndrome has not disappeared, and there persists widespread opposition in the public, in the armed forces and in religious circles to going ahead with the campaign to overthrow the Sandinistas. No matter how popular Reagan is as a president, he has not been able to sell the 'contra' cause at home – even by going to the extraordinary length of proclaiming himself a 'contra' and hailing the contras as 'the moral equivalents' of 'the founding fathers'.

But the pressures to unleash military power remain intense. One effect of the Libyan attack is that it sabotaged the effort to reduce presidential authority to act alone by requiring advance consultation with Congress. Another may be to generalise the response and make of it a retaliatory strategy that docs not require concrete justifications or authorisations.

Somewhere it is necessary to admit that the left in Europe and the United States has been baffled by the terrorist phenomenon and as a result has come off looking badly. In the background are leftist sympathies for the moral and political grievances which animate terrorist activity. The left is also on guard against efforts to use anti-terrorism as a mandate for anti-democracy. We in the United States noticed how willingly Congress waived its prerogatives, feeble as they are, to jump on the pro-attack bandwagon. The Reagan people wasted no time, introducing legislation the day after the raid that would give the President an exemption for anti-terrorism from the War Powers Act, including even a legitimate option to dispatch without authorisation a hit team to assassinate foreign heads of state suspected of terrorist sponsorship.

The issues are complex. Many terrorist groups espouse their cause in a political language that owes much to Marxism. Radical intellectuals associated with these groups are themselves products of European education and immersion in radical politics during their student days. The public, then, notices that the left is silent about terrorism and suspects complicity. In my view, there exists on the left confusion and inhibition rather than much sympathy for the practice of terrorism. One consideration is a reluctance to reinforce reactionaries, which extends to its anti-democratic, militarist associated agenda.

But what then does the left propose? To oppose military action of Reagan's sort is coherent, and even sensible, but it is not a counter-terrorism policy. If terrorism persists and receives endorsement and support from foreign leaders, then the societal demand for action grows irresistible. Fear, frustration and rage make punitive military action a popular option even if, as we have seen with the Tripoli attack, it is perceived as inciting additional terrorist activity. Merely to stand against this tide is to lose legitimacy. A coherent and serious alternative view is required.

A counter-terrorist programme for progressives

Without attempting to spell out a complete programme, this could include: 1) a reasoned moral and political repudiation of terrorism directed against innocent persons as an instrument of struggle; 2) a call for the repudiation of state-sponsored terrorism on all sides of political conflict, including, especially, that of high-technology states; 3) a critique of prevailing US anti-terrorism programmes as calculated to cause fear and intimidation in the general public leading both to interventionism and to the breakdown of democracy; 4) a call for positive action on Third World grievances which have generated terrorist tactics in the past; 5) support for counter-terrorist law enforcement which relies on prudence, plays down media rewards and strengthens international law.

1) Repudiation. The repudiation of terrorism must be, first of all, on moral grounds: to kill deliberately for political goals is, at best, an absolute last resort; to kill innocent civilians is never acceptable no matter how acute the injustice. In any event, such tactics mobilise and legitimate repressive tactics. These tactics generally work against the satisfaction of grievances, but, through media exposure, may be the only way on to the political agenda. Hence, terrorism can 'work' even if it sets back overall prospects for solutions. For this reason repudiation is not enough. A credible mechanism is required for the pursuit of the moral and political claims of the oppressed and aggrieved.

Further, our repudiation of terrorism must not be simplistic or self-righteous. After all, Europeans and Americans look back on resistance activity against the Nazis as heroic, even if civilian targets were attacked. Zionist terror undoubtedly accelerated the British departure from Palestine. We have to acknowledge that there are certain situations in which 'terrorism' has been admired by the West and others where it has been effective in reaching the goals of its practitioners. Such acknowledgement may clarify the moral and political complexity of the issues, and overcome the tendency to proceed from repudiation of terrorism to repudiation of the Third World as a whole, or to suppose that recourse to terrorism is the behaviour of 'barbarians'. Political violence by the oppressed is not terrorism if the objective of attack is a military or property target. The ground of debate then shifts to the broader issue of violence in political struggle, and, if the dominating side is using indiscriminate violence, acts of resistance may assume a more defensive character.

Despite these qualifications, the repudiation of terrorism must be forthright and genuine. To kill Olympic athletes, to hold schoolchildren hostage, to silence political opponents in foreign societies by illicit assassination – none of these are ever acceptable as a tactic of struggle. Nor is the overall intention to provoke widespread fear by producing spectacles of blood-curdling violence suitable for prime time TV and tabloid extras.

2) First World Terrorism. The propagandists of modern states do their best to hide their own reliance on terrorism and to associate its practice with Third World revolutionaries and their First World leftist sympathisers. The manipulation of political language is a powerful weapon in perpetuating this deadly fraud. By and large, 'terrorism' is reserved to describe the tactics and methods of the weak, while the indiscriminate violence of the strong is portrayed or glorified under labels which hide its terroristic character.

The use of high-tech weaponry and tactics are not classified as 'terrorism' even when refugee camps are the targets and women and children are the victims. Typical First World tactics are to send planes or to rely on naval artillery and missiles to inflict pain and devastation. This is an extension of the one-sided wars of the colonial and pre-colonial eras where virtually all casualties were on the weaker side. In the post-colonial era, the use of planes and ships to terrorise Third World adversaries is standard practice. It underscores the facts of one-sidedness. There is 'legitimate' means for the Third World to retaliate, to make the First World share their vulnerability. It is not surprising that jet planes and airports are favourite targets for Third World groups. These symbols of high-tech mobility penetrate the cultural and physical space of low-tech societies, who expose their vulnerability and make the rich societies shudder. Terrorism on all sides is about making 'the other' feel vulnerable, and if the First World wants to end Third World terrorism it had better put a stop to its own high-tech terrorism and the interventionary politics that underlie it. A first step is to realise the terrorist character of high-tech military operations.

In the background there is inevitably the role of nuclear weapons in security. This weaponry of mass destruction is the most terrifying in our historical experience. The graveyards of Hiroshima and Nagasaki remain prime exhibits of state terrorism. Ronald Reagan, as an aspiring Rambo of anti-terrorist militancy, is also the propagator of the Star Wars delusion, the ultimate high-tech fix which promises to leave the entire world, except the United States, vulnerable to the will and whim of American crisis managers. SDI is the final mad terrorist fantasy, but it hides its sinister implications behind the language of deterrence and defence. It obscures the fact that it is practising on a far grander scale the same terrorism that it labels 'barbaric' under Gaddafi's sponsorship. The moral and political hypocrisy is most blatant in respect of such 'freedom fighters' as the 'contras' in Central America or the UNITA irregulars in Angola. To sponsor such violence against the civilian populations and legitimate governments of foreign countries is to adopt terrorism as a policy. Who is to say whether these CIA wars are more or less terroristic than terrorist incidents by revolutionary groups? Certainly, the former kill more civilians. What can be said is that unless the First World renounces state-sponsored terrorism it will be whistling in the wind if it calls upon the Third World to do so. The weak are not about to give up unilaterally the one means they have of making the First World feel the vulnerability they experience as a common lot (not only militarily, but economically as well, via indebtedness, multinationals' manoeuvres, capital flows, and the like).

When the US Secretary of State publicly advocates ' "disruptive" covert operations' against Libya as he did on CBS TV on 27 April, he is violating the golden rule of diplomacy, that is, claiming a right for the United States which he would not for a moment grant to other states. As such, it is a breach of the most fundamental tenet in the state system as it denies the notion of sovereign equality. Everyone realises that there are gross disparities in geopolitics, but to convert those disparities into prerogatives is to erode the fragile consensus among governments that makes moderate statecraft possible. As such, it plays into the hands of those who hold extremist and nihilist views and who insist that violence and military power are the only solutions for international conflict. It is this feature of the American approach that is, perhaps, most disturbing of all.

At the same time, it is evident that the practice of terrorism is deeply embedded in First World technology and politics. Terrorism is at the heart of both interventionism and nuclearism, and to repudiate state-sponsored terrorism is probably a lot harder for Reagan and Thatcher than for Gaddafi and Khomeini. So we must not make the convenient assumption that we can get rid of the latter while retaining the former.

3) Critique. Only 23 Americans were killed as a result of terrorist incidents in 1985 which is 'about one-fourth the number who die each year as a result of being struck by lightning'. Apart from the bomb explosion in the US military barracks in 1983 which killed 241 Marines (more plausibly regarded as an act of war rather than an incident of international terrorism), in no year of the

1980s did US fatalities due to terrorism rise above the level of 25. This is well below the number of homicide victims reported for any one of the 20 largest cities in the US. In 1984, worldwide, 597 terrorist incidents were recorded, with more than 300 deaths and 1,000 or so wounded. These are bloody statistics, of course, and the cumulative trend is upwards, but the risks of injury remain infinitesimal for the average citizen, and hardly provide grounds for shuddering in fear behind closed doors. If a friend or neighbour changed travel plans for fear of lightning we would assume s/he was nuts. Why, then, the extraordinary media hype reinforced by an impression of dire danger in official circles?

Might not the exaggeration be useful to leaders unwilling to deal with difficult issues of social distress at home? As Walter Karp has brilliantly demonstrated in *The Politics of War*, it has been standard practice for American presidents to create foreign diversions in the face of economic downswings and high domestic unemployment. During recent years, when both American political parties have essentially given up on welfare or compassionate capitalism, there have been a variety of festering wounds at home, especially in the inner cities. The struggle against terrorism pushes these issues out of political consciousness.

In the United States, there is a conviction that a successful foreign policy depends on bipartisan support, moral enthusiasm, and a vivid, menacing enemy. The Vietnam War shattered the consensus which had underlain Cold War foreign policy. The hope now among official ideologists is that anti-terrorism will provide for foreign policy in the 1980s what anti-communism did in the 1950s and 1960s. Even more grandly, the US leadership of counter-terrorism on a worldwide basis can be seen as re-establishing US claims to exert leadership in a world situation of growing diplomatic isolation and intra-capitalist rivalry. Washington's effort to turn the Tokyo economic summit into a counter-terrorist prayer meeting illustrates this.

Then, too, the terrorist spectacle is deliberately staged as a kind of theatre of the grotesque. Whether it be tossing an aged, handicapped Jew overboard in his wheelchair or gunning down tourists waiting for their boarding passes, the staging of terrorism is aimed at capturing the political imagination. In this respect, the statistics do indeed understate the reality. The fascination with the grotesque so present in modern civilization makes such tactics especially productive. Terrorism as 'news' and terrorism as 'entertainment' are uncomfortably close.

These suppressed motivations need to be exposed so that the threat of terrorism is reduced to proper proportions. This is itself a contribution to counter-terrorism. After all, the terrorist strategy is to maximise fear by exaggerating the threat to public order, as well as to expose the vulnerability of even strong, rich societies to the anger and exploits of the weak. There is an odd convergence of motives between the terrorist who seeks to paralyse the adversary society and the counter-terrorist who seeks to mobilise that society in support of unilateralism and retaliatory violence. To break these linkages is crucial.

One observation stands out. If we seek to deprive terrorist activity of its impact, and therefore weaken the incentives to practise it, then we must put its exploits in proper context, and provide reassurances about safety and security. No counter-terrorist politics can succeed unless they include an appreciation of why terrorist preoccupations have gripped the body politic to such an extent.

4) Positive Foreign Policy. The most effective US counter-terrorist approach would arise from a foreign policy which took the sufferings of others seriously. This would contrast with official counter-terrorism which views suffering as irrelevant, or even as the reason to inflate the terrorist danger. More concretely, whatever the motives of governments which sponsor terrorism, their capacity to recruit terrorists and to glorify their deeds rests on widespread public support for their moral claims. To put the issue more concretely, if the Reagan administration really wanted to put a stop to most varieties of Mediterranean terrorism it would use its diplomatic and economic leverage to work on behalf of Palestinian self-determination and do its best to give the PLO a sovereign state. The basic rationale for Palestinian statehood rests on the Palestinians' identity as a people in a specific territory and their struggle to express that identity in a political form. They deserve to share territory and resources in the region with Israel, and some kind of co-existence based on mutual rights is the only genuine path to peace and justice.

Of course, such a foreign policy would not be credible unless it grew out of domestic values and practices, and did not arise as an afterthought once the terrorist challenge was already being experienced. Further, to pursue counter-terrorism abroad in a credible manner presupposes a commitment to the challenges of suffering at home. Counter-terrorism that goes beyond the level of gestures profoundly challenges the overall ethos of capitalist civilisation, and possibly, of secularism and militarism. The terrorist challenge is so difficult because an appropriate response requires so much of us.

5) Law Enforcement. Law enforcement has a place in counter-terrorism. It should be easier to mobilse intergovernmental co-operation to identify and prosecute terrorist suspects. Extradition could be made more effective. An international criminal tribunal could be established which held the commission of terrorist acts an international crime.

British and American progressives find themselves captive of official policies which abet militarism and terrorism. Their struggle must be to create a climate of opposition which at least inhibits official policies. Prospects are better in Britain than the United States. The Democratic Party is an enfeebled opposition. There is no immediate prospect of principled opposition. At the same time, there are deep doubts in grassroots America about the overall quality of political leadership. A movement is waiting to be born here.

At the same time, radical neo-conservatives are riding high. They have emerged from the Libyan affair as harsh critics of the Atlantic alliance. They believe that Euro-American collective diplomacy weakens the US capacity to act decisively in the world. They dismiss Europe as too decadent to fight for its own interests, and question whether the US should remain burdened. Ironically, Jeanne Kirkpatrick has sounded a note to stem the tide of anti-alliance feelings in high places, pointing out that a government which joins an alliance has not lost its independence beyond the strict limits of the alliance relationship. In the case of NATO, this obliges the allies to collective mechanisms of response to Soviet military action in Europe, but nothing else.

Any sharp Euro-American rupture would undoubtedly strengthen the Reaganite disposition toward global unilateralism and militarist foreign policy. We should strengthen the Euro-American ties at the popular level of social movements. In this sense, the issue of terrorism belongs on the agenda of the peace movements in both regions, and co-operative efforts are needed to explore whether a stance on counter-terrorism can be developed which would win international backing.

THE VIEW FROM OXFORD STREET

E. P. Thompson

When the F-111s took off from British bases on the night of 14/15 April to bomb Tripoli, this signalled that Britain had been relegated to the Third Division – a little oil-state in the north-eastern Atlantic, or a bomber platform much like Diego Garcia in the Indian Ocean or Guam in the Pacific.

The British had joined the wogs of the Third World, and would have to make up their minds whether they were of the deserving and loyal or the bad kind. It was not much consolation to know that Mrs Thatcher had been nominated for an Oscar by the White House as the Third World's Most Loyal Wog of the Year.

It also signalled that it was time for the British peace movement to examine its strategies and perspectives. Some thousands of us had a chance to do this for an hour or so, while sitting peacefully in Oxford Street on Saturday 19 April.

I am still not sure how we came to be there. CND's national office had been inconvenienced in its organisational calendar, since the Americans had perfidiously chosen to bomb Libya in the very week when CND was launching its Basic Case campaign. It had already had to postpone the Basic Case once, because of the Fulham by-election. It could not do that again.

However, CND responded well to the calls which jammed its switchboard, and summoned a sitdown at the US Embassy in Grosvenor Square on Saturday 'from 12 to 4 pm'. Since I had managed to find this out by ringing the switchboard, and had advertised the event in a *Guardian* Friday 'Agenda' piece, I turned up promptly at noon. (I should explain that while I am one of a number of vice-presidents of CND, this is an ornamental and honorary post without rights, and outside CND's policy-making structures.)

It was a nice, well-policed, and self-policing affair. The police had effectively barricaded off the whole embassy (as was to be expected) and we were allowed to sit down or stand, as we chose, in the two streets on both sides of the square. Those who wished to testify by NVDA (why is the peace movement getting as acronymic as the war movement?) could do so by sitting on the road and getting wet bottoms.

CND members as well as non-badge-wearing members of the general public (NBWGPs) – many of whom had come in from the West Country, the Midlands, Wales or East Anglia – had come prepared for more than that. No one wanted a punch-up with the police. (Well, maybe 0.01% did.) But most had come expecting to offer a passive symbolic obstruction which could result in arrest.

Such CND stewards as there were had no guidance to offer. Nor had I. We got a leaflet saying we were to sit down until four, and then rise all together and sing a verse from a hymn.

In fact, nearly everyone had risen by 2 pm to try to dry their bottoms. Grosvenor Square became a social event, with people wandering around and greeting friends. At 2.30 I slunk off with Dorothy and two friends to get a cup of coffee. Returning to the square soon after three, we were amazed to find it almost empty. People had not waited on their bottoms to sing a hymn. They had voted with their feet to go down Oxford Street and join another demonstration in Hyde Park. We took off in the same direction.

To our surprise we found Oxford Street at a standstill, with several thousand people sitting down on some hundreds of yards of London's main artery. The pavements, at the week's peak shopping hours, were packed with mingled non-sitting demonstrators (NSDs) and interested (non-hostile) shoppers (NHSs). Since this seemed to be the wisdom of the moment, we concurred by sitting down.

This was clearly an Unlawful Act, and (worse) it might have been an offence to Selfridges' Saturday afternoon turnover. But it seemed to be a way of making a point. It was also a chance to meditate and to have political discussions. One of my neighbours turned out to be an eel-fisherman from the River Wye. I gathered that, because of the foul spring, the eels were not rising or mating (or whatever should be seasonable). So far as the eels were concerned, it would make no difference if he sat in Oxford Street for the next few weeks.

The wisdom in our section seemed to be that we would sit there until the police moved us on, or at least until our buses to the provinces were due to go back. The few police around were good-humoured, and clearly were as unprepared as we were. After an hour or so, police reinforcements arrived and they started budging the buses both ways down Oxford Street and moving (or throwing) the demonstrators out of their way.

If you are sitting down you cannot see far in any direction. I was told later that there were punch-ups and examples of aggro in one portion of the crowd. I am sorry if this was so. In my own section I saw not one single example of aggression or violent resistance by any member of the sit-down. My own section seemed to be divided, like Swift's Little-Enders and Big-Enders, between those who took different views of the rules of 'tag'. One party assumed that as soon as the police put a hand on their shoulders and told them to move on – or actually dragged them out of the way of the buses – they were 'out'. The other party assumed that you weren't 'out' until you were actually arrested, so, however many times you were shifted, you could get back on the road and go limp once more.

This must have been aggravating to the police, since some of us, when limp, are pretty heavy, and since they didn't have the vans around to arrest hundreds of us. And perhaps some of the police were frightened by our numbers and visible determination. This may explain why we were at the receiving end of quite a bit of aggro. People had their arms and necks twisted, I got boots in my back, Dorothy would have had her shoulder dislocated (alack, by a policewoman, with two pips, an Irish accent and no number) if some women in the sit-down had not restrained the policewoman. I saw a friend – a Warwickshire farmer with a gammy leg – being thrown on to the edge of the pavement, and the eel-fisherman was carried off by his feet and both *ears*, just in time to get the bus back to Hereford.

At the same time, if you sit down in the capital's main shopping street, you expect to come away with an arrest or with one or two bruises. Several of the police who lugged me around were solicitous and quite gentle. I put the violence down (as CND did in its press statement) to a politically motivated minority.

I will reserve further details of this astonishing event to my forthcoming handbook on NVDA. (Mem: when going limp, keep your neck down, keep your hands clenched – so that your fingers can't be broken – and keep your temper.) The interesting question is, why did this spontaneous sit-down happen?

There are various explanations: it was a brilliant coup by the Socialist Workers' Party (but there were only 40 to 50 of them around); or it happened because the police started splitting up the procession on the pretext of letting traffic through (probably true of the actual occasion when the sit-down started). My own explanation is that the peace movement had come to a point when it found itself possessed by an uncontrollable urge to do something it has managed to restrain itself from doing for several years: that is, to sit down for an hour or two and *think*. And if my explanation is wrong, then it is certainly time for it to do that now.

The peace movement had no reason to expect that Libya, terrorism and terroristic F-111s were suddenly going to be tipped into its lap. After a slow start and a screech of changing gears (from the Basic Case), national CND did well. Many local CNDs, as well as many other groups, did very well, as a hundred (mainly unreported) actions around the country and at US bases testified.

What raised questions for the peace movement was the new situation in which we find ourselves; and the need for initiatives alongside or as well as CND. CND is a single-issue campaign, and its middle name is 'nuclear'. It is also a national movement: the 'nuclear' means getting nuclear weapons out of Britain. To this, various other issues are from time to time added at annual conferences, but they remain marginal to the nuclear 'Basic Case'.

There is nothing wrong with this, and very much that is right. With my whole heart I hope that CND will maintain itself and prosper, as a nationwide association of persons united on this basic anti-nuclear premise. It cannot take on 101 other issues on which its supporters are not united, although these supporters may be the heartland from which other initiatives will come.

But someone must take on these issues. And there are a great many of them, which do not fit easily into a 'nuclear' frame, nor into a frame which is far more concerned with national policy than with international relations. How does one define as a 'nuclear' issue the US-inspired terror against Nicaragua, the war in Afghanistan, the unending series of crises in the Middle East, the problem (and the new Soviet proposals) regarding conventional armaments in Europe, the fulfilment of the Helsinki agreement?

I do not think that a great part of the British people were roused to indignation by the bombing of Tripoli out of fear that this would tip us into nuclear war. The dominant feelings were not of fear but of outrage and shame: outrage at the bombing of a sleeping city, and shame that it had been done from our own bases. Of course there is a nuclear connection: the F-111s, the bases, the exacerbation of the Cold War. But to reduce the Libyan crisis to a 'nuclear' question is a thin view of things. In a thicker view, so many issues are raised – the arms trade, relations between the advanced and the Third World, the unresolved problems of the Middle East, the independence and integrity of this nation – that they engage with opinion far wider and broader than even broad CND.

This is to emphasise that there is both a need for other initiatives, dealing with other issues, and a space for them to inhabit. Insofar as most issues lead us back eventually into a nuclear frame, the raising of them can only strengthen CND's case. What would be wrong, in CND, would be to arrogate to itself the pretence that it is the *only* peace movement and *all* the peace movement; that its single issue is the only issue worth devoting time and money to; and that the solution to all problems will be found in building its own central organisation bigger and bigger. The movement can be stronger only if centres of initiative are diversified. We also need a diversity of voices, and of regional and political accents. If every voice has to be sanitised by going through a series of committees and issuing out as the authorised view of an authorised spokesperson, then the voice will become muffled, repetitious and in the end boring.

It is interesting to note how, even in the matter of peace movements, nations revert to national type. In the individualistic US there is a plethora of little organisations, which manage to get together in common actions or coalitions. (I was once at an event in San Francisco, where there were 80 or 90 people; we went round the room and found that 127 different organisations were represented, each with its own 'constituency' and sometimes its own global solution.) In Italy, there was a time when a peace meeting could be the dreariest thing imaginable, since each leftist political faction had the right to make a highly theoretical statement as to its own position on everything. In West Germany, the peace movement is fissioned into SPD, Greens, church movements, women's, communist and so on, which have loud public debates with one another, but generally manage to work out a common platform and plan of action. In Greece, each section of the divided left appears, in effect, to have its own peace movement. In Norway, there is an umbrella movement, No to Nuclear Weapons, rather like CND, and tilted a bit towards the left, the trade unions and Christian pacifists. In vast Canada, the regionally based movements have an extreme suspicion of any attempt to centralise the movement and control it from Toronto or Ottawa. In Spain, all initiative and all power rests with the local autonomous communes, and full-time peace staff don't exist.

Most of these methods are, as Mr Podsnap would have said, 'Not English'. It is perhaps because of our weather that the British have a liking for umbrellas. Also, we have a 'genius for compromise'. Give the British half a chance, and they will form themselves into a body shaped like an umbrella, with an annual conference, arrangements committee, amendments, points of order, rulings from the Chair, and motions of 'next business'.

CND, in this, is as British as you can get. The lineage of CND's annual conference goes directly back to forebears like the Methodist Conference, the TUC and several political parties. It is a doleful, ritualistic occasion, an expensive diversionary exercise, which (elections apart) has little influence on what the movement actually does; most initiatives – Cruisewatch, peace camps, Snowball – spring up outside the conference hall. Little sectarian factions hop about in the conference like fleas; unable to gain support for their policies in their own right, they come here to fatten off the peace movement's blood. Each tries to attach its own issue, by devious amendments, to the single issue of CND . . . but I won't go on.

CND is proud of being British in this way, and often points out that we have a United Movement, unlike Other Nations. And long may Conference rule over us. Yet something is lost as well as gained. In other nations, the peace movement can be seen to be made up of diverse tendencies and voices, sinking their differences in a larger common issue. A running debate goes on before the public, as to strategies, priorities and international developments; and this goes on all the year round, and not only once a year in a formal ritualistic way. Hence serious political debate is encouraged, not only within the movement but among the public. There are confusions and frictions within it, but the movement gains the authenticity of open argument.

CND is a single-issue, non-party (or any-party) organisation which for some reason has saddled itself with all the paraphernalia of a political party. I regret this. I would prefer it if we acted as an alliance or a coalition, and stopped trying to pretend to be a uniformity which we don't have. This will not lessen my support for CND. But it enforces the need for alternative centres of initiative and, above all, of open political discussion. Action-directed peace groups are fine, but if we do not also have greater opportunities for informed debate, our peace movement will spend all its energies dealing with symptoms instead of causes. The cult of unanimity at all costs can simply be a charter to any pig-headed faction, however small – such as the discredited 'tankies' around the *Morning Star* – to veto all discussion (even of the sources of the Cold War itself) on the grounds that it is 'divisive', i.e. it rubs the fur of their taboos the wrong way.

Among the many organisations which merit support alongside CND (such as the Campaign against the Arms Trade, the National Peace Council, the United Nations Association or Amnesty) I will now advocate the cause of European Nuclear Disarmament or END.

END is now six years old. Its first appeal was issued by a group of us, in association with the Bertrand Russell Peace Foundation, on 30 April 1980. This was an international appeal, signed by thousands across Europe and beyond, to get nuclear weapons and bases out of Europe, and also to campaign to break down the bloc system, East and West: that is, to campaign not only against nukes but against the condition of the Cold War itself.

We took up an explicitly non-aligned position. That is, the Cold War will not be ended by the victory of one side or the other, but only by a mobilisation of citizens on both sides to overcome its armaments and ideologies. The hegemony of both superpowers must, by peaceful means, be rolled back – of the Americans over West Europe and of the Soviet Union over East Europe – and a healing process between the blocs must commence.

END, as an organisation and as a London office, was formed over five years ago to advance these aims. Our major activities were: publications (*END Journal*, published every two months, is the best-informed peace movement journal anywhere); public meetings of an international character; and the work of communicating, monitoring and translating. The results of this time-intensive and expensive work have been made available to the entire peace-concerned public. We have raised our own finance from the donations and bankers' orders of a small group of loyal supporters, from the royalties and sales of publications, from friends in the US, from the generosity of artists or musicians, from sales and auctions, and very deeply from our own pockets.

END is not a single-issue organisation. It is a political organisation, with distinct policy guidelines: an intervention in the Cold War. We try to respond to major international issues as they arise. We start, not from Britain (we support CND's policies here) but from the divided continent of Europe. Every strategy to break down that division concerns us: military, political, economic, cultural, nuclear or conventional disarmament, zones of disengagement, a neutralised Mediterranean, nuclear-free zones in the Baltic or the Balkans, East-West citizen exchanges, and the dialogue between Christians, East and West.

Although a small organisation, we have made a large input into the discourse of British and international political life. From the original END appeal and *Protest and Survive*, to Star Wars and the Libyan crisis, our ideas have influenced action and been heard by world opinion. We were the first to make contact with similar movements in Europe and to build up a transnational alliance in opposition to cruise, Pershing and SS-20s. We quickly built relations with the United States Freeze movement and other American voices for peace. Our members and supporters visited East Europe, and made direct contacts, not only with formal (state-endorsed) peace committees but also with independent peace groups and voices; this led to fruitful relations with the influential human rights group, Czechoslovak Charter 77, the Trust Group in Moscow, circles of Hungarian students and youth, independent women in East Germany, and the new 'Freedom and Peace' group in Poland.

This work has been brought to a wider public by a stream of publications – *END Journal, END Churches Register* and pamphlets published in association with Merlin Press. We now have specialist groups which monitor developments in countries – East, West and Third World – translate materials and make these available to the public. We have helped to build up the North Atlantic Network, which brings together nations around the Atlantic seaboard in common actions and conferences. We are also, in co-operation with other organisations, developing forces in the Third World and in China. Together with CND and Quaker Peace and Service, we have made a major input into the annual END conventions, in Brussels, West Berlin, Perugia, Amsterdam and (this year) Paris. We see all this work as being something more than saying 'no' to nukes: it is actively building the infrastructure of peace by improving citizen relations and understanding, fostering common strategies and saying 'yes' to an undivided world.

This work, continued over six years, has stretched our small resources to the limit. In the first years, by a self-denying ordinance, we did not build an active membership, at the request of other peace organisations, who thought this could lead to competition and confusion. We thus cut ourselves off from a major source of support, advice and renewal. Last year we became a membership organisation, while other organisations, by affiliating to END, may draw on our services and take part in our work. Yet we have found that we have been around so long that our work is taken for granted – even many of those who warmly support our initiatives have been slow to become members or dig into their pockets. We are now really short of money, in need of more active supporters, and even in danger of losing our office and our gifted and overloaded staff. If readers have long intended to join END, the time to do so is now.

These were some of my meditations while sitting in Oxford Street. The world is now too complex and too dangerous for us to be content to just say 'down with nukes'. And despite all the generous investment of time and spirit, we are not getting rid of them. Despite all the talk about a 'Geneva spirit', not one single act of disarmament is taking place. The American and British governments have responded to the more flexible diplomacy of Mr Gorbachev as if it were some kind of threat. The long-sustained unilateral test ban moratorium of the USSR was answered by continued US testing (with British support), while the answer of France was to sink the *Rainbow Warrior*. Every time a younger generation of Soviet leaders make an initiative, President Reagan and Mrs Thatcher slam the door, with Soviet fingers trapped inside it.

Is this because the peace movement is dealing with only half of the problem? For five years it has been gingerly skirting around the core of the problem: the Cold War itself. Unilateralism, multilateralism, Freeze – none of these can get to the heart of that, unless we add to them a strategy to break down the blocs, encourage trust and exchanges between citizens, loosen the NATO and Warsaw Pact alliances, and undermine the power of the Cold War ideologists and of their military and security structures.

This requires political strategies and political debate, which END exists to further. END offers, not an alternative to existing organisations, but an addition, an international dimension and a clear direction. Month by month the profile of direct US domination is rising over West Europe, and in Europe the resentment is rising also – the Atlantic is growing wider. With the bombing of Libya, the US kicked over the traces of NATO and gave a new meaning to the word 'unilateralism'. In Washington today 'unilateralism' is an in-word, and it signifies the right of the US to use its military muscle as it chooses, and to bombard or bomb without consulting its allies, even in the heart of Europe, the Mediterranean Sea. At the same time, Star Wars is being forced upon us, both as an endless protraction of exotic military measures and as an instrument of US control over our industry, with the imposition of new security screens.

We now know – if we did not know before – how savage will be the US response, if a government were to be returned at the next election which had the nerve to remove their cruise missiles or nuclear bases. (Yet neither the opposition political parties nor even CND have begun to seriously debate the political situation which will then disclose itself.) All this leads us towards the need for common action and common strategies with our West European neighbours, in the effort to get out from under US hegemony. Yet get out in which way? Towards a West European mini-superpower, or towards a new affirmative *Ostpolitik* and new non-exploitative relations with the developing world?

At the same time the Soviet Union is signalling more flexible diplomacies; and Mr Gorbachev has now taken up one of END's earliest demands, for the pull-back of Soviet and American nuclear *and* conventional forces, 'from the Atlantic to the Urals'. Is this propaganda? Bluff? Or is a space at last opening, in which European peace forces might put our broken world back together?

These questions are all political questions, which require both information and political discussion. That is why END needs money and members, and why the peace movement (and British political life generally) needs END. Up and down the country we need centres for informed political debate and international contact. These may be END groups, or, if you prefer, existing organisations, affiliated to us, drawing on our services and giving back to us their support and advice. If the F-111s can fly from British bases to bomb Libya, then the British peace movement must answer them by getting out and about the world. Certainly, we shall do all in our power to close those bases down. But what if the US then starts behaving 'unilaterally' towards us? We shall stand in need of friends, just as our friends stand in need of us. We cannot close down the Cold War on our own.

APPENDIX OF TABLES

ARMS SALES TO NORTH AFRICA ($mn 1975 prices and exchange rates)

Suppliers	US	France	UK	Italy	Other NATO	USSR	Other Warsaw Pact	Others	Total
Recipients									
LIBYA									
1970-74	46	441	30	10	–	130	–	1	656
1975-79	60	361	6	94	–	3311	40	40	3911
1980-83	18	112	–	637	44	2020	27	22	2879
EGYPT									
1970-74	–	11	8	–	–	2152	27	–	2197
1975-79	99	256	146	14	1	477	–	14	1007
1980-83	2842	302	111	114	69	–	159	1	3598
REST OF NORTH AFRICA									
(Algeria, Morocco, Tunisia = the Maghreb)									
1970-74	45	52	–	16	8	6	3	–	129
1975-79	336	956	30	37	48	726	2	13	2149
1980-83	460	287	18	81	97	331	–	10	1283

Source: SIPRI Arms Trade Registers, unpublished.
NB SIPRI arms trade statistics are not comparable with US ACDA figures.

MILITARY EXPENDITURES IN THE MEDITERRANEAN 1975 – 1984
(US$mn at 1980 prices and exchange rates)

	1975	1976	1977	1978	1979	1980	1981	1982	1983	1984
Albania	93.3	112	115	117	126	131	134	134	[130]	. . . . .
Greece	2288	2508	2658	2715	2630	2276	2693	2746	2500	2710
Italy	7728	7687	8257	8608	9154	9578	9781	10463	10689	11435
Portugal	2870	3295	3173	2906	2578	2442	3015	3296	3172	3051
Spain	3297	3529	3538	3526	3699	4007	4101	4650	5071	5280
Turkey	2870	3295	3173	2906	2578	2442	3015	3296	3172	3051
Yugoslavia	2641	2734	2784	2742	2937	3134	2950	(2638)	(2551)	[2365]
EUROPE	21787.3	23210	23698	23520	23702	24010	25689	(27223)	[27285]	[28022]
Cyprus	31.2	30.4	39.3	31.4	40.5	30.9	44.8	[48.1]	[68.6]	. . . . .
Egypt	[4267]	[3711]	[3882]	[2179]	[2068]	[1464]	[1488]	[1679]	[1883]	[1944]
Israel	(4441)	(4433)	(4431)	(3943)	(4155)	(4256)	(4565)	(4382)	. . . . .	. . . . .
Lebanon	91.7	95.2	74.2	143	215	332	308	363	426	. . . . .
Syria	1390	1409	1387	1506	2511	(2144)	(2018)	[1841]	[1995]	[2140]
MIDDLE EAST	[10220.9]	[9678.6]	[9743.5]	[7802.4]	[8989.5]	[8226.9]	[8090.8]	[8313.1]	[8622.6]	. . . . .
Algeria	597	837	729	792	783	890	792	829	909	894
Libya	[1310]	[2142]	[2461]	[3113]	[4045]	[3276]	[2475]	[2182]	. . . . .	. . . . .
Morocco	676	948	1088	966	971	1118	1140	[1511]	[1329]	[803]
Tunisia	95.7	118	161	181	178	194	223	296	(307)	(315)
North Africa	[2678.7]	[4045]	[4439]	[5052]	[5977]	[5478]	[4640]	[4818]	[4745]	[4212]
TOTAL	34680.9	36933.6	37880.5	76474.4	38668.5	37714.9	38419.8	40354.1	406252.6	[40734]
United States	139277	131712	137126	137938	138796	143981	153884	167711	179615	200839

Source: *World Armament and Disarmament SIPRI Yearbook 1985*, London: Taylor & Francis, 1985.

. . . . . Not available   ( ) Estimate   [ ] Uncertain estimate

MILITARY EXPENDITURES, ARMED FORCES AND ARMS TRADE IN THE MEDITERRANEAN 1983

	Military Expenditures $mn	Military Expenditures as a share of GNP	Armed Forces Thousand	Armed Forces per 1000 people	Arms Imports $mn	Arms Imports as a share of total of imports	Arms Exports $mn	Arms Exports as total exports
EUROPE								
Albania	188*	7.8+	53*	19.6*	0	0	0	0
Greece	2526	6.2	177	17.9	470	4.9	0	0
Italy	9609	2.7	498	8.8	170	0.2	1000	1.4
Portugal	814	3.5	93	9.3	50	0.6	60	1.3
Spain	4070	2.1	340	1.2	200	0.6	340	1.7
Turkey	2840	4.9	824	16.7	600	6.4	230	4.0
Yugoslavia	2309	3.7	259	11.4	130	1.1	320	(3.2)
MIDDLE EAST								
Cyprus	(83)	3.6	10	14.3	20	1.6	0	0
Egypt	(2679)	8.3	447	9.8	1700	(19.0)	50	(1.7)
Israel	(6229)	29.0	180	45.0	370	3.8	220	4.3
Lebanon	437	8.2	419	9.6	240	6.5	0	0
Syria	(2138)	13.0	222	22.7	1700	43.7	30	1.6
NORTH AFRICA								
Algeria	(1334)	2.7	130	6.3	350	3.3	0	0
Libya	(4223)	17.5	5	19.4	1900	25.7	70	0.6
Morocco	1318	8.2	135	5.9	320	8.9	0	0
Tunisia	(256)	2.9	28	4.0	40	1.2	0	0

Source: US Arms Control and Disarmament Agency, *World Military Expenditures and Arms Transfers 1985*, Washington DC: USACDA, August 1985.

( ) Estimate * 1981 latest available figure + 1979 latest available figure

VALUE OF ARMS TRANSFERS 1979-83, BY MAJOR SUPPLY AND RECIPIENT, IN THE MEDITERRANEAN ($MN)

Supplier	Total	USSR	US	France	UK	West Germany	Italy	Czecho-slovakia	China	Romania	Poland	Others
EUROPE Total	6245		3025	620	35	1380	265				80	835
Greece	1985		900	60	10	300	110				80	525
Italy	635		600	5		10						20
Portugal	260		100		10	130						20
Spain	1500		675	550	10	90	5					170
Turkey	1865		750	10	5	850	150					100
Yugoslavia	690	480	40	20	10		10					130
MIDDLE EAST Total	21120	9720	6470	1515	625	250	340	470	390	20	85	1065
Cyprus	55			5								50
Egypt	5645	40	2400	1200	575	210	320		300		50	550
Israel	3805		3800									5
Lebanon	395		250	90	10		10				5	30
Syria	10530	9200		200	180	40		470	90	20	30	300
NORTH AFRICA Total	17925	9000	540	1960	95	705	1525	575	320	310	280	3320
Algeria	3660	3200		30	50	300						80
Libya	12095	5800		850	40	380	700	575	310	310	230	2900
Morocco	1785		430	950		5	50				50	300
Tunisia	385		110	130	5	20	70		10			40
TOTAL	**27365**	**18720**	**10595**	**4075**	**765**	**2335**	**2130**	**1045**	**710**	**330**	**445**	**5220**

Source: US Arms Control and Disarmament Agency, *World Military Expenditures and Arms Trade 1985*, Washington DC: USACDA, August 1985. These figures should be treated with caution. They appear to underestimate European arms exports and overestimate Soviet arms exports.

FOREIGN TROOPS IN THE MEDITERRANEAN 1985

	United States	United Kingdom	France	West Germany	Turkey	Greece	Libya	Syria	Israel	Iran	USSR	East Germany	Cuba
EUROPE													
Gibraltar		2040											
Greece	2900												
Italy	10170												
Portugal	1080			800									
Spain	12000												
Turkey	3880												
MIDDLE EAST													
Cyprus		4810	17000	1750									
Egypt	1,500												
Lebanon							800	25000	200	650			
Syria											7000	210	
NORTH AFRICA													
Algeria											1000	250	
Libya											1800	400	3000
Morocco	. . . . .												
TOTAL	**31530+**	**6850**		**800**	**17000**	**1750**	**800**	**25000**	**200**	**650**	**9800**	**860**	**3000**

Source: Ruth Leger Sivard, *World Military and Social Expenditures, 1985*, Washington DC: World Priorities Inc, 1985.

MILITARY BASES IN THE MEDITERRANEAN AREA

ITALY	
* Aviano AB	US rotational F-4 aircraft on nuclear alert.
Catania, Sicily	Italian 'Atlantique' ASW patrol aircraft to be supplied with US nuclear depth bombs.
* Comiso	US Ground Launched Cruise Missile (GLCM) main operating base.
* Gaeta	HQ, US Sixth Fleet, destroyer tender.
* Ghedi-Torre AB	Italian Tornedo base with US nuclear weapons custody.
* La Maddelena	US attack submarine training and refit site, with submarine tender.
* La Speiza	NATO ASW training and research centre.
* Naples	Central NATO command HQ in Italy, including Allied Forces Southern Europe (AFSOUTH) and US Naval Forces. Europe (NAVEUR).
Rimini AB	Italian F-104 base with US nuclear weapons custody.
* Sigonella, Sicily	US ASW operating centre, P-3 ASW base, and nuclear weapons supply point for US Sixth Fleet.
Tavorara, Sardinia	NATO very low frequency (VLF) transmitter to US subs in Meditteranean.
Teuluda	NATO VLF transmitter to Meditteranean.
Vicenza	HQ, Southern European Task Force (SETAF), and US artillery group.
PORTUGAL	
Montijo	Part-time rotational US P-3 ASW aircraft stating base.
Oeiras	Commander, Iberian Atlantic (BERLANT).
FRANCE	
Hyeres AB	Airbase for Super Etendard squadron.
* Istres AB	Mirage IV A base and nuclear weapons storage site. Aerial refuelling aircraft.
La Regine	Low frequency transmitter to French ships and submarines in Mediterranean.
* Toulon	Naval base, homeport for French aircraft carrier.
GIBRALTAR	
Gibraltar	Commander, Gibraltar Mediterranean Command Gibraltar guardship (UK), naval base & dockyard supporting ships which carry nuclear-capable ASW helicopters. Airfield used by UK Nimrod aircraft.

GREECE	
* Araxos AB	Greek F-104 base with US nuclear weapons in custody.
Athens	Commander, Eastern Mediterranean (NATO/AFSOUTH).
Canea, Crete	NATO missile firing range used for Lance.
* Elefsis	HQ, US artillery groups with central nuclear storage rotational.
Hellinikon AB	US strategic reconnaissance planes (RC-135) US strategic communications site.
Kato Souli	US low frequency (LF) transmitter to submarines in Mediterranean.
Prevenza	Forward operating base for NATO AWACS aircraft.
Souda Bay, Crete	Part-time rotational US P-3 ASW staging base.
SOVIET UNION	
Batumi	VLF transmitter to Soviet submarines in Black and Mediterranean Seas.
Feodoysia	Submarine base, Black Sea Fleet.
Guardeskoye AB	Naval Backfire base supporting Black Sea Fleet (could be at Oktyabirski).
Krasnodar	VLF radionavigation transmitter.
Odessa	HQ, Odessa Military district Air Army.
* Oktyabirski AB	Naval Backfire basc supporting Black Sea Fleet.
Palkiski	Homeport for Golf 11 submarine.
Saki AB	TU-22 Blinder base supporting Black Sea Fleet.
Sevastopol	HQ, Black Sea Fleet, naval and submarine base.
SPAIN	
Rota	US ASW operating centre, P-3 aircraft staging base.
Torrejon AB	US Sixteenth Air Force strategic communications site.
Zaragoza AB	US aerial tanker base, strategic communications site.
TURKEY	
* Balikesir AB	Turkish F-104 base with US nuclear weapon custody.
* Erhac AB	Turkish F-104 base with US nuclear weapon custody.
* Eskisehir AB	Turkish F-104 base with US nuclear weapon custody.

* Incirlik AB	US rotational F-4 aircraft on nuclear alert.
Konya AB	Planned forward operating base for UK Nimrods assigned to NATO Airborne Early Warning (NAEW) force.
* Murted AB	Turkish F-104 base with US nuclear weapon custody.

* Indicates locations where nuclear weapons are routinely stored.

WARS AND WAR-RELATED DEATHS IN THE MIDDLE EAST AND MEDITERRANEAN SINCE 1945

		Number of Deaths		
	Date	Civilian	Military	Total
SOUTHERN EUROPE				
Greece Civil War; UK Intervention	1945-49	. . .	. . .	160000
Turkey Terrorism; military coup 1980	1977-80	. . .	. . .	5000
MIDDLE EAST				
Cyprus, Nat. Guard v. Makarios, Turkish Invasion	1974	3000	2000	5000
Egypt Suez, France, Britain and Israel invading	1956	0	3000	3000
Egypt Six-Day War, Israel invading	1967-70	50000	25000	75000
Iran Islam v. Shah; Islam v. dissidents	1978-83	17000	0	17000
Iran Iraq Invasion; territorial dispute	1980-82	. . .	27000	27000+
Iraq Shammar tribe v. govt	1959	1000	1000	2000
Iraq Civil War; Kurds v. govt	1961-70	100000	5000	105000
Iraq Iran attack; fol. Iraq invasion	1982-	. . .	. . .	400000+

		Number of Deaths		
	Date	Civilian	Military	Total
Israel invasion by Arab league	1948	0	8000	8000
Israel Yom Kippur War; Egypt, Syria invade	1973	0	16000	16000
Jordan, Palestinians v. govt, Syria invade	1970	1000	1000	2000
Lebanon Civil War; US intervening	1958	1000	1000	2000
Lebanon, Muslims v. Christians; Syria intervenes	1975-76	75000	25000	100000
Lebanon, Israel invasion v. PLO and Syria	1982-85	8000+	17000	25000+
Syria, govt massacre of Sunni Muslims	1982	10000	0	10000
Yemen, Yahya family v. govt	1948	2000	2000	4000
Yemen, Civil War following coup; Egypt intervening	1962-69	. . .	. . .	101000
NORTH AFRICA				
Algeria Civil War; France intervening	1945	2000	0	2000
Algeria, War of Independence	1954-62	160000	160000	320000

		Number of Deaths		
	Date	Civilian	Military	Total
Algeria, former rebel leaders v. govt	1962-63	1000	1000	2000
Morocco, War of Independence from France	1953-56	3000	0	3000
Tunisia, War of Independence from France	1952-54	3000	0	3000
West Sahara, War of Independence from Morocco	1975-85	3000	7000	10000

Source: Ruth Leger Sivard, *World Military and Social Expenditures 1985*, Washington: World Priorities, Inc., 1985.

Only includes wars with deaths of more than 1000. Does not include Libyan intervention in Chad, in 1980.

ARMS SUPPLIES TO LIBYA

Date	No.	Item	Supplier	Comment
		AIRCRAFT		
1959	2	Auster AOP.5	UK	Ex-RAF
1959	2	Heliopolis Air Works Gomhuriah	Egypt	
(1959)	2	Bell 47J	US	
(1962)	3	Sud Alouette I	France	
1963	2	Lockheed T-33	US	Gift
1964	1	Douglas C-47	US	
1965	5	Douglas C-47	US	
1966	1	Lockheed T-33	US	
1968	5	Northrop F-5 Freedom Fighter	US	
1969	5	Northrop F-5 Freedom Fighter	US	
1969	1	Lockheed C-140 Jet Star	US	
1970	8	Lockheed C-130 Hercules	US	
1971	20	Fouga Magister	France	
1971	1	Dassault Falcon	France	
1971-72	4	Aérospatiale Alouette III	France	
1971-72	9	Aérospatiale SA.321 Super Frelon	France	
1971-74	58	Dassault Mirage 5	France	
1971-74	32	Dassault Mirage IIIE	France	Some were on loan to Egypt during October war of 1973
1971-74	20	Dassault Mirage IIIB/IIIR	France	
1975	29	MiG-23B 'Flogger' fighter aircraft	USSR	Arms: 4 Atoll AAM
1975-76	12	Mil Mi-8 helicopters	USSR	
1976-81	20	Marchetti/Boeing Vertol CH-47L Chinook helicopter	Italy	
1977-78	12	Tupolev Tu-22 'Blinder'	USSR	Arms: 'kitchen' ASM
1977-78	38	Dassault Mirage F-1 A/B/C Air combat fighter	France	Arms: Matra 'Magic' AAM

Date	No.	Item	Supplier	Comment
1978-79	110	SIAI – Marchetti SF-260W Warrier Trainer/COIN aircraft	Italy	Delivery prior to licenced production
1978	1	Bell-121 helicopter	US	
1978	5	MiG-25 'Foxbat' strategic reconnaissance aircraft	USSR	Flown by Soviet pilots
1978	1	Cessna-421C Trainer	USSR	
1978	1	Lockheed Jetstar-2 Transport	USSR	
1978	100	L-39 Albatross Trainer	Czecho-slovakia	
1978-80	24	Mi-24 Hind D helicopter	USSR	According to Arab sources, Libya was first non-WTO customer. Reportedly flown by Soviet pilots
1978-83	70	G-2Ae Soko Galeb armed trainer	Yugoslavia	
1979	40	SA-342K Gazelle helicopter	France	
1979	1	Agusta AB-212 helicopter	Italy	
1979	10	DHC-6 Transport	Canada	
(1979-81)	130	MiG-23 fighter strike aircraft	USSR	Includes 18 'Flogger-F' strike aircraft flown by Cuban and East German crews
(1979-81)	(60)	MiG-25 fighter aircraft	USSR	Arms: 'Acrid' AAM
1981-83	20	G-222L transport	Italy	
(1981)	(190)	MiG-21 'Fishbed' interceptor/attack	USSR	
1981	2	C-130 H Hercules transport	US	
1980-81	(100)	SU-20/22 Fitter – E/F/J fighter/ bomber	USSR	
1980-81	6	SA-321GM Super Frelon	France	
(1980-81)	2	Agusta A-109 Hirundo helicopter	Italy	

Date	No.	Item	Supplier	Comment
1982-	8	Fokker-27 MK-600 transport	Netherlands	May be for civilian use
1983	(12)	Mi-14 'Haze' helicopter	USSR	For ASW
(1982-3)	(60)	SIAI-Marchetti SF-260W Warner trainer/COIN aircraft	Italy	
1984	10	Let L-410 transport	Czechoslovakia	
(1983)	(3)	An-26 'curl' transport	USSR	
?	10	Cessna 0-1 Bird Army observation aircraft	Italy	
?	6	AB-476 helicopter	Italy	
?	5	AB-206 Jet Ringer helicopter	Italy	
ON ORDER				
	(8)	Embraer EMB-111 Marine Patrol Craft	Brazil	
	25	Embraer EMB-121 Xingu transport	Brazil	
	(100)	Embraer EMB-312 Tucano trainer	Brazil	
	20	CH-47C Chinook helicopter	Italy	
	. . .	G-2AE Galeb Trainer/Strike	Yugoslavia	
		MISSILES		
1968-69	(48)	Nord SS.12 (M) ATM	France	To arm patrol boats
(1972)	300	BAC Vigilant ATM	UK	
1973	(18)	Short Seacat SHAM	UK	2 triple launchers on Mk 7 frigate
1973	3 bat.	Matra/Thomson-CSF Crotale SSM	France/S. Africa	Developed in France to South African specifications with 85 per cent South African funding
. . .	3 bat.	Matra R.550 Magic AAM	France	On order; to arm Mirage
1975	3 bat.	K-13 'Atoll' AAM to arm MiG-23	USSR	
1975	3 bat.	AT-3 'Sagger' ATM	USSR	'large number being supplied according to US intelligence'

Date	No.	Item	Supplier	Comment
1974-75	3 bat.	SA-2 SAM	USSR	Total 62 launchers; first displayed on military parade, 1974
	3 bat.	SA-3 SAM		
	3 bat.	SA-6 SAM		
1976	3 bat.	Thomson-CSF-Matra Crotale SSM	France	
1976	25	SS-1 'Scud' tactical battlefield support SSM	USSR	With non-nuclear warhead; displayed on military parade
?	45	SS-1 'Scud' SSM	USSR	
1976-77	. . .	'Kitchen' SSM	USSR	To arm Tu-22
1976-77	288	SS-N-2-'Styx' Sh Sh M	USSR	To arm 24 'Osa' class missile boats
1977-78	(232)	R-550 Matra Magic AAM	France	To arm Mirage F-1
1977-78	120	MM-38 Exocet Sh Sh M	France	
1979-83	(168)	Matra/Oto Melara OTOMAT	France/ Italy	To arm 4 missile corvettes under construction in Italy
(1979-81)	. . .	AA-6 'Acrid' AAM	USSR	To arm MiG-25
1980-81	12	SS-12 'Scaleboard' Landmob SSM	USSR	
1981-84	(12)	SA-N-4 Sh AM	USSR	To arm Nanuchka class corvettes
1981-83	(48)	SSN-2 'Styx' Sh Sh M	USSR	To arm Nanuchka class corvettes
1983	(36)	SSN-2 'Styx' Sh Sh M	USSR	Land-based version to protect Gulf of Sidra
(1984)	(12)	Otomat-2 Sh Sh M		Arming frigate 'Dat Assawari' after retrofit in Italy
1985	. . .	SA-5 'Gammon' SAM	USSR	Deployed at Surt, on Gulf of Sidra
?	?	SA-7 SAM	USSR	
?	?	SA-9 SAM	USSR	
ON ORDER				
		Otomat-2 Sh Sh M	Italy	Arming new 'Wadi' class corvettes
. . .	. . .	Matra R.550 Magic	France	On order, to arm Mirage
		NAVAL VESSELS		
(1962)	3	Fast patrol launch	UK	For customs and fishing
1963	2	Inshore minesweeper 'Ham' class	UK	Displ: 120 t; ex-British; lent 1963; given outright 1966

Date	No.	Item	Supplier	Comment
1966	1	Corvette, 'Tobruk'	UK	Displ: 400 t; completed 1966
1966	1	Maintenance repair ship	UK	Displ: 657 t; ex-British
1967	2	Coastguard vessel	UK	Displ: 100 t; new
1968-69	3	Fast patrol boat, 'Susa' class	UK	Displ: 95 t; new; armed with SS.12 SSMs
1968-69	4	Coastguard vessel	UK	Displ: 100 t; new
1969	1	Logistic support	UK	Displ: 2200 t; new
1969-70	4	Patrol boat, 'Garian' type	UK	Displ: 100 t; new
1973	1	Frigate Mk 7	UK	Displ: 1325 t; new; armed with Seacat SAMs
(1976)	4	'Agosta' class submarines	Spain	
1976-77	5	'Osa' class fast patrol boats	USSR	Arms: Styx
1976-77	3	'Foxtrot' class, ex-USSR submarines	USSR	
1978-81	4	'Assad' class missile corvette	Italy	Arms: OTOMAT
1978-82	7	'Osa' class fast patrol boats	USSR	Arms: Styx
1981	1	'Foxtrot' class submarine	USSR	
1981	2	'Natya' class ocean minesweepers	USSR	Ships named Ishssan and Tayyar
1981-84	4	'Nanuchka' class corvettes	USSR	
1982-84	10	'Combattante II' CMN fast/attack missile patrol boats	France	Arms: Exocet ordered in 1975 but delayed owing to war in Chad; ban lifted in July 1981
1982-84	4	'Natya' class ocean minesweepers	USSR	
ON ORDER				
	4	'Assad' class corvette	Italy	To be armed with OTOMAT; rearmed Assad class
	4	'Koncar' class first attack air-craft	Yugoslavia	Unconfirmed; based on Swedish Spia design; armed with Styx

Date	No.	Item	Supplier	Comment
		ARMOURED FIGHTING VEHICLES		
1957	(10)	Centurion tanks	UK	
(1960-61)	(15)	Saracen	UK	
(1960-61)	(40)	Saladin	(UK)	
(1962-63)	(15)	M-113	US	
(1966)	(15)	Ferret	UK	
(1966)	(15)	Shorland	UK	
1970	36	BTR-50	USSR	
(1970)	(15)	T-34	Egypt	
1970-71	(200)	T-54/55	USSR	
(1972)	(15)	BMP-76	USSR	
1972-73	170	M-113	Italy	Ex-Italian
. . .	(200)	Tanks	UK or France	Order for British Chieftain from 1969; reportedly cancelled; French AMX-30 ordered instead
1974-75	600	T-55/T-62 Tank	USSR	Received by Sept 1975
(1976)	(2000)	T-62/64 Tanks	USSR	According to US intelligence
1976-77	200	T-72 Tanks	USSR	
1978	200	Engesa EE-9 Cascarel Armed recce car	Brazil	
(1979-80)	(200)	Eugesa EE-11 Urutu armed patrol car	Brazil	Used in military operation 1980
1980-	200	Lion Main Battle Tanks	Italy	
1982-84	210	Palmaria 155/141 Self-propelled Howitzer	Italy	
ON ORDER				
	210	EE-11 Urutu armoured patrol car	Brazil	
	210	EE-9 Cascarel armoured car	Brazil	
	210	EE-TI Osorio Main Battle Tank	Brazil	
	(30)	Dana 152 mm self-propelled Howitzer	Czecho-slovakia	

. . . Not available
AAM Air to Air Missile
ASM Air to Surface Missile
ASW Anti-Submarine Warfare

ATM	Anti-Tank Missile
COIN	Counter Insurgency
SAM	Surface to Air Missile
SSM	Surface to Surface Missile
Sh Sh M	Ship to Ship Missile
S Sh M	Surface to Ship Missile
	Quotation marks are used for name of class of naval vessel, and for NATO code name for USSR weapon systems.
Sources:	Stockholm International Peace Research Institute (SIPRI) *Arms Trade Registers with the Third World* (Stockholm: Almqvist and Wickseel, 1975); *World Armament and Disarmament, SIPRI Yearbook 1976, 1977, 1978, 1979, 1980, 1981, 1982, 1983, 1984, 1985*, London: Taylor & Francis, 1976-85.
	International Air Forces and Military Aircraft Directory, Essex: Aviation Advisory Services.

OTHER BOOKS FROM PLUTO

THE FATEFUL TRIANGLE
Israel, the United States and the Palestinians
NOAM CHOMSKY

From its establishment as a Jewish state until the present day, Israel has enjoyed a special position in the American roster of friends and enemies.

The Fateful Triangle is a definitive study of the complex and explosive politics which revolve around this relationship, and the attitudes of both Israel and the USA towards the Palestinians.

In exploring the world's most dangerous flashpoint, Chomsky identifies the peculiar workings of modern nation-states, and their war and media machines.

A work of scholarship and a superb political polemic, *The Fateful Triangle* will be a central, and highly controversial, work in discussions of international politics for years to come.

'Maybe the most ambitious book ever attempted on the conflict between Zionism and the Palestinians viewed as centrally involving the United States.' *London Review of Books*

492 pages
0 86104 741 9 £7.95 paperback

REAGAN AND THE WORLD
Imperial Policy in the New Cold War
JEFF McMAHAN

This book is a scathing indictment of Reagan's foreign policy. It pierces the screen of official rhetoric and propaganda to reveal the real motives for the behaviour of the United States under Reagan.

El Salvador, Nicaragua and Grenada are the latest in a long list of countries in which the USA has intervened. The object is to bolster the USA's command of Third World resources and to protect American big business.

The nuclear arms build-up is intended to frighten the Soviet Union away from any interference with USA interventionist policies around the globe.

'A scathing indictment of Raygun and his policies. Frank Allaun. *Tribune*

224 pages
0 86104 602 1 £3.95 paperback

INSIDE CENTRAL AMERICA
US Policy in its new Vietnam
PHILLIP BERRYMAN

Central America could be the Vietnam of the 1980s and the war is already on. Washington plans the bombing of the Salvadorean rebels. The anti-Sandinistas are organized and funded by the CIA. Between one and two million Salvadoreans and Guatemalans have become refugees and tens of thousands of Central Americans have been killed in the 'Americanization' of the war.

This book looks at the way the USA has acted in the region, the way in which it has forced East/West geopolitics on to a deprived, colonized people who are fighting for ordinary freedoms, and the way in which it is determined to preserve a repressive status quo.

A must for all those who want the truth about Central America.

176 pages
0 7453 0109 6 £3.95 paperback

ZAPPING THE THIRD WORLD

The Disaster of Development Aid

MARCUS LINEAR

Aid has become our new imperialism. We have mountains of grain while the Third World starves.

In our desperate search for cheap hamburger meat we use deforestation and chemicals to destroy the Third World's ecology. We ruin their economies by ramming our agribusiness machines and techniques down the throats of their farmers. The FAO and other 'aid' institutions are the bureaucracies we build on the backs of the world's poor.

This book sets out the case, gives concrete examples of our 'aid' and is bitter in its criticism. However, it also describes ways in which the Third World can fight back.

256 pages
0 7453 0013 8 £4.95 paperback

SIZEWELL REPORT

What Happened at the Inquiry?

MARTIN INCE

Who needs Sizewell? Can we afford it? Is it safe? These are among the questions that the public enquiry into the new power station at Sizewell is supposed to answer.

This book describes the enquiry, looks at the evidence, and calls in question many of the assumptions made by the industrially interested parties.

Sifting through the mountain of evidence presented at Sizewell, Martin Ince has written a combative first 'report'.

'A concise and readable account.' *New Statesman*

224 pages
0 86104 627 7 £3.95 paperback

FORTRESS SCOTLAND

A Guide to the Military Presence

MALCOLM SPAVEN

The history, politics and geography of Scotland force on it a key role in preparations for war in Europe and the North Atlantic.

From radar stations to nuclear weapons stores, this book details the acitivities and roles of over 200 military installations in Scotland. It explains Scotland's role in US and NATO strategy and reveals the disturbing impact of the military presence on the people, economy and landscape of Scotland.

Published in association with Scottish CND.

208 pages. Illustrated
0 86104 735 4 £3.95 paperback